Warm Bricks at My Feet

Warm Bricks at My Feet

A Danish Immigrant Family's Struggles and Triumphs through a Uniquely Challenging Period in 20th Century America

Marian Love

iUniverse LLC
Bloomington

WARM BRICKS AT MY FEET
A Danish Immigrant Family's Struggles and Triumphs through
a Uniquely Challenging Period in 20th Century America

iUniverse books may be ordered through booksellers or by contacting:

iUniverse LLC
1663 Liberty Drive
Bloomington, IN 47403
www.iuniverse.com
1-800-Authors (1-800-288-4677)

Because of the dynamic nature of the Internet, any web addresses or links contained in
this book may have changed since publication and may no longer be valid. The views
expressed in this work are solely those of the author and do not necessarily reflect the
views of the publisher, and the publisher hereby disclaims any responsibility for them.

Any people depicted in stock imagery provided by Thinkstock are models,
and such images are being used for illustrative purposes only.
Certain stock imagery © Thinkstock.

ISBN: 978-1-4917-3002-7 (sc)
ISBN: 978-1-4917-3003-4 (e)

Library of Congress Control Number: 2014905699

Printed in the United States of America.

iUniverse rev. date: 04/08/2014

I dedicate this book to loving memories of the special people in my life including my parents, loved ones, and especially to my children and their families. It has allowed me to revisit joys and regrets and to always be reminded of the journey we each take.

This memoir would not have come to fruition without the hard work, persistence and encouragement from my son-in-law, Andrew Goldstein. My appreciation and gratitude are everlasting.

Table of Contents

Part 1: My Parents 1
Part 2: My Siblings 31

Family Photographs..83

Part 3: My First Marriage 109
Part 4: My Second Marriage 115

Appendix A 127
Appendix B 129
Index 131

Part 1

My Parents

Part 1 presents my parents' adventures and struggles both in Denmark and in America. They immigrated to the United States twice, failing to gain a foothold as Iowa farmers after their first journey and returning to Denmark. But circumstances compelled them to return once again, a little older and more experienced but still destined to confront struggles from within and outside their growing family. The journeys of their ten children led, in most cases, to very different lives.

My father, Anders Christian Andersen, was the fourth of eight children; he was born on January 6, 1876, a cold winter's day, in the coastal village of Scøttrup Børglum in Jutland, the mainland of Denmark. Scøttrup Børglum was inhabited by tough, independent small-acreage farmers and fishermen. My mother, Mariane Olivia Christensen, was born on June 11, 1885, in the northwestern village of Lønstrup, also in Jutland. She was the fourth of ten children. She always had such lovely skin; even at her birth, her father compared it to the manna from heaven that God had provided for the Jews. The name Manna stuck with her all of her life.

My parents came from very different backgrounds. My mother's father was a highly successful metalsmith. He provided his family with a good income and a nice home. The family's earlier home was smaller, but owing to his financial success, they bought a lovely, large home. Both homes still stand in Jutland. My mother's home was very chaotic. Her parents provided the best possible material comforts, but her mother was an extremely moody person with wide swings in her personality. She demanded perfection but was unable to enforce her demands. One evening when my grandparents were gone, one of my mother's brothers, Chris, grew restless, and wanting to impress his siblings, he loaded a pistol muzzleloader with a candle, aimed it at a door, and blew a large hole through it. My mother would recount the fear she felt when she was told to do her studying but instead chose another more pleasant task. When her mother unexpectedly walked in on her and discovered that she was not studying, my mother fainted from the fear of being caught disobeying her mother.

My grandfather Christensen was a patient man who tried to maintain peace both at home and in his work. He often charged less than the going rate for the work he did or chose to collect no payment at all, depending on the individual's ability to pay. My grandmother would get furious with him and often was compelled to take things into her own hands, demanding payment for my grandfather's work. In her up moods, she would bake goodies to take to her friends and neighbors. She was determined to provide her children with the best of everything. Twice a year, a seamstress came to their home to sew the clothes she wanted for her family. Despite her efforts to protect her children, two of her brothers, Herman and Elias, still suffered serious injuries. My uncle John accidentally drove a pitchfork through his younger brother Elias's leg. Although Elias developed osteomyelitis, he gave credit to the quality of his medical care, as well as to an aunt who came to his rescue by feeding him in the hospital. He credited his aunt for his recovery. When he left the hospital, he herded geese for her while his leg completely healed.

Herman, a younger brother of my mother, fell in the barn as a young man, sustaining an injury that left him with a hunched back. His brother Gudmund, the youngest among my mother's brothers, developed tuberculosis later in life. I remember admiring a very handsome picture of him. My sister Eva's son, Jim, looked very much like Gudmund. My mother's brother Jens Christian was the oldest of my mother's siblings. During World War II, he helped American flyers escape from Denmark to Sweden using his boat. He was a fisherman off the west coast of Jutland. On one occasion, he encountered Nazi patrol boats off the Danish coast as he returned from his rescue missions, but he was able to talk his way out of the encounters.

Among my mother's attributes was a playful streak, and she enjoyed fun and mischief wherever she could find or create it. On one occasion, she and her sister Marie convinced their younger brother John to bury his money, convincing him that, like planting seeds on the farm, the coins would multiply and increase in value. Sometime later, John decided to harvest his growing treasure, only to become angry and desperate when he found nothing. He eventually realized what had happened and proceeded to assault his sisters with his wooden shoes.

My mother loved the ocean and took every opportunity to bring my grandfather his lunch while he served as a rescuer in the Danish coast guard. He would aid ships in distress off the Danish coast, a common consequence of the stormy weather there. My grandmother often chose to send the children to bring their father his lunch because of her fear of the seas.

My mother recalled the fun she had when she and her girlfriends stripped naked one day and entered the ocean off the Danish coast. While they were frolicking in the water, some young men gathered and refused to leave as they anxiously awaited a better look at the young girls when they emerged from the water. My mother said the bravest of her friends acknowledged she had nothing to hide, and so she was the first to walk out of the water followed by the rest of them.

My grandfather Andersen's name was Jens. He was the ninth of eleven children and the only son. Five of his siblings died in infancy. It was said that my grandfather was accorded special preference in the family, and as a result, he inherited his father's farm from his mother. My father's mother was named Ane Kirstine Laustdotter. She was confirmed in 1858. She received high marks in primary and secondary schools for both her good knowledge and virtuous behavior. My paternal grandfather started his marriage at the farm he inherited. During the early years of their marriage, my grandparents were known to have parties that lasted well into the morning hours, with the guests' horses still tied to posts when the sun came up. Not surprisingly, the liberal consumption of alcohol and my grandfather's alcoholism became well known throughout the local community. Jens Andersen was a selfish and demanding husband who often came home drunk and was abusive to his wife. When my father was old enough, he dared to confront his father and finally took him to task, shouting at him that he would never allow abuse of his mother again in his presence.

Grandma Ane Kirstine was stricken with various health problems and eventually died of tuberculosis. As a child, she suffered from kyphosis, a curvature of the upper spine, and my father in anger called her a "hunchback." With deep guilt later in life, he shed tears as he shared his sadness for having described his mother in these terms, saying it was his greatest regret.

At the age of ten, my father was taken to a farm by his father, where he was hired out as a servant, herding cattle in the field and having to sleep in the barn with an older farmhand. He remembered his father, Jens, taking him to the farm where he was to go to work. Jens emphasized to the farmer not to hold back on any punishment of my father. While telling me the story, my dad said he thought to himself, *Aren't fathers supposed to protect their children?* One night my father was struggling to breathe during an attack of croup. He began praying for help, and the other hired hand, hearing his labored breathing with forced words of prayer, asked what was wrong. Given this bleak existence, he looked forward to the moments when he would see his mother walking through the fields to see him. He recalled catching a glimpse of her in the distance and running to her as fast as he could, overjoyed for the moment. My father was allowed to spend a few hours a week with his family and was paid only five Danish kroner every year.

One day, my father found a rabbit that had just been killed in the field. Delighted, he ran home to give it to his mother to cook for the family. He used up his lunchtime, so he had to go without a meal. My dad worked herding cattle until he was fourteen years old; then he was given a suit of clothes and allowed to go to school for a few years, but he never finished high school. Instead, he was hired to finish the year teaching at the grade school, where the older boys were incorrigible and drove the headmaster to literally jump out a window. But being such a strong and determined man, his first encounter with teaching resulted in the quick reestablishment of order in the classroom.

My father later joined the Danish cavalry and was always very proud whenever he talked about his military talents. Pictures of him in uniform show a large sword at his side. My brother Henry remembered his father's demonstration of swordsmanship. As a result, Henry and my other brothers practiced sword-fighting with large sticks and later proudly showed off their talents to my father.

My father chose the career of a brick mason and was admired as a perfectionist in his work. It was during a remodeling job for my mother's parents that he first saw my mother. He was smitten by her from then on. When he first saw Mariane walk by him, he was impressed with her beauty. Her sister Marie, who was two years older and not as attractive, walked by later. My father thought he was mistaken in his first impression of my mother. Later, when my mother walked by again, he was no longer able to contain his feelings. He reached out to her and pulled her close to his chest, telling the other workers that this was the way to hold a beautiful lady, "close to your heart." My mom was embarrassed, but from that moment on, she could think of no other man but my father. Shortly thereafter, having finished remodeling their home, he began pursuing her. She was only fourteen years old, and my grandparents forbade her to see him. This resulted in a three-year ongoing battle between my mother and her parents. My grandparents did not like the fact that my father was ten years older, and, worse, he was the son of an alcoholic. They sent her away to stay with her aunt Karen and her grandmother. She was never out of their sight. One Sunday morning as they arrived at church, her aunt was on one side and her grandmother on the other. My mother was squeezed between them in the pew. Noticing my mother's predicament, the minister took pity on my mom. During his sermon, he told her to have hope as she sat there in the pew, caught between a falcon and a hawk.

My mother had a friend named Minnie who came to her aid. Minnie brought paper and a pencil to a toilet where my mother would write notes to my father. Minnie delivered the notes to her aunt, who then gave them to her husband Jens who made the final delivery to my dad. Jens in turn would deliver notes from my dad back to my mother in the same manner. After this went on for a while, my grandparents decided that this secretive communication could not continue, so they sent my mother away to live with her sister Ane Kirstine and her husband. However, my parents discovered another way to communicate, by leaving a nail in a specific location to alert my mother of his presence.

During an altercation that started when my father was found outside hoping to see my mother, my grandmother was overcome with such anger that my grandfather swung his cane at my father, striking him on his forehead. My grandfather turned to my grandmother, asking if she was now satisfied, and then told my mother to clean him up. With eyes filled with tears as my mom bandaged my father's head, she said to him, "Don't worry; they will never keep me away from you!" Given my grandparents' disdain for my father, my parents realized they would never be free to see each other, and so they began making plans to go to America.

My father came from an insecure home, and so he cherished the dedication and love he received from my mother. He had strong attachments to his mother, who was no longer living, having died at the age of fifty-four on January 28, 1897. He had vivid memories of her having to give up his younger sister Tina at the age of only three years old to leave for America with her brother Martin, who was twelve. My father, who would have been fourteen at the time, remembered with great sadness the day when Tina and Martin left. His mother wept as they departed, for she could only have faith in the care they would receive. My father told her he could run to stop them before they boarded the boat. But she answered, "What's the use? I cannot take care of them." My dad remembered three-year-old Tina running to get her mother's slippers for her. Martin died from diphtheria two years after leaving for America. His caretakers were Seventh-Day Adventists, who sang Christian songs believing God would save him if it was his will. Before Martin died, his caretakers told him that he had been a good boy and was therefore assured a place in heaven. Martin replied that he was not always a good boy, because he would on occasion steal a lump of sugar from the pantry. My dad remembered Martin coming to him in a dream at the time he died.

Tina lived with the hope that she would someday see her mother again. She was seven years old when she received word from Denmark that her mother had died. She was overcome with grief and had no one to comfort her broken heart. She went to the outhouse and wept until her caretaker came, scolding Tina and saying that her crying was not going to bring her mother back and that she should dry her tears and come back inside.

Money was scarce as my parents planned their escape to America, so they needed to find the money for my mother's boat ticket. My father was able to borrow money from a friend, and so the date was set for their departure. My mother was back home again, and her worry turned to how she would escape without her parents discovering her plan. Before departing, she wrote a letter explaining that she had departed Denmark with my father, Chris, and was on her way to America. Her parents received the letter after Chris and my mother departed. On the night she left, my father raised a ladder to her upstairs window. She climbed down and joined him without awakening her parents. It must have been a breathtaking moment for them. I can only imagine my grandparents' reaction, having repeatedly failed to isolate my mother from Chris, only to discover that, in an instant, she was beyond their control. Shock and grief must have turned into lasting anger. At one time while they were in America, my parents were in desperate need of help. My mother wrote her parents asking if they could borrow money, but they refused her plea. However, they continued exchanging letters.

My mother described her feeling of panic after they boarded the boat, realizing that, although she was no longer a prisoner kept isolated from my father, she was completely cut off from her parents' help. Now she had to put her full faith in my father. They arrived in the United States in May 1903 as foreigners in a strange new country, unable to speak a word of English. They took some comfort knowing there were a few Danish relatives in America who they hoped would provide some degree of security until they could establish themselves. My father had an older brother, Lars, who left Denmark for America at the age of seventeen. Lars bought a farm and was relatively successful. Fortunately, Lars's wife, Aunt Julia, who had seven children, was a very kind, loving woman and provided friendship and support that my mother desperately needed.

My father's first job in America was working on the railroad for ten cents an hour. My mother was able to earn fifty cents a day doing laundry for a local doctor. As poor as they were, their first order of business was to pay back the loan for my mother's ticket to America. My father had great pride and was deeply hurt when he was made the butt of his fellow workers' jokes. He began longing for the days back in Denmark, where he was well respected.

Despair overtook my mother, and she turned to God. They were Lutherans, but only the Methodist church offered sermons in Danish. My mother said that after she developed her great need for God, she became a changed person. She read the Bible from cover to cover and always quoted passages to her children. I don't believe she would have survived without her newly acquired strong faith. My father shared with me that he and my mother prayed together during the years when they were apart in Denmark. I remember my dad trying to console me when my first husband, Bart, a World War II bomber pilot, was declared missing in action. He shared with me the value of the strength they received when my parents prayed together during the hard times. He asked me whether Bart and I prayed together, believing it would give me strength. In my early youth, my brother Ken and I took turns reading nightly from the Bible. My father had no specific ritual, but he occasionally asked all of us to stand and recite the Lord's Prayer.

My parents were married in September 1903, four months after arriving in America. They were living in Missouri Valley, Iowa, struggling to make ends meet. My dad's hope was to buy a farm like his brother Lars had, but he was becoming discouraged. Uncle Lars offered one of his cattle sheds as a temporary home to my parents. My sister Eva was born on September 22, 1904. Keeping her warm and healthy while living in a shed was a major challenge. She was only a few months old when they moved into the shed. It was very cold in the winter, and the floors were bare concrete. My mother scrubbed and cleaned the shed as best she could, but the foul odors increased as the weather turned warmer. It was no surprise that Eva was sick a great deal of the time.

Aunt Julia and my mother became very good friends. Julia was a casual housekeeper. She allowed chickens to wander into the house. Uncle

Lars worked his sons very hard, as well as his horses. I was told about the day he called his sons from the field to bring over another horse because their horse Prince had just dropped dead.

My aunts Paulina (aka, Mettine Pouline) and Tina (aka, Attine Marie) became close to each other after Paulina came to America. They were visiting Julia when they were asked to help out because Julia had just given birth. They refused saying that they needed the time to practice singing Christian hymns in the woods so they could become missionaries. My mother brought Eva to Julia's house while she did the work that had to be done. She was frustrated and angry with Paulina and Tina for refusing to help Julia, saying their refusal was nonsense and their priorities were out of line.

Uncle Lars was the first in his family to come to America. He was by all accounts an unusual character. He actually spanked his younger siblings when he was about to depart Denmark, thinking that a good spanking would stop them from feeling sad that their brother was leaving. Once in America, Uncle Lars provided much humor to the family. My older brothers and sisters told me about the many hours having fun being with him. Uncle Lars was fun-loving and provided lots of entertainment just being himself. He loved eating all manner of sweet things. One day he found a bowl of Jell-O prepared by Aunt Julia, who had placed the bowl on the windowsill to cool. The Jell-O was not yet firm when Uncle Lars sampled it. It was so irresistible that he proceeded to consume the entire bowl, complimenting Julia by saying, "That was one doggone good goody drink!" As was often the case, she became frustrated whenever Lars was unable to control his impulses. Her response to Uncle Lars was, "My conscience Louie, that was my Jell-O you just ate!"

On another occasion, thinking it was a special treat for Aunt Julia, Uncle Lars took her to the county fair and then left her to conduct his business in town. When his work was completed, Lars hurried home to take care of the farm chores. As he walked in the door, he called for Julia and became increasingly frustrated when no one answered. Suddenly, as if a light went on in his head, he exclaimed, "By golly, I think I left her at the fair!"

On one special occasion, Lars had the opportunity to ride a roller coaster. He was probably talked into doing this by one of his older sons. He had no idea what he was getting into and later recalled it as a near-death experience. He screamed, "Stop this machine!" but to no avail. He then waved a five-dollar bill in the air hoping he would get the attention of someone who would help him. He was convinced he would die and never see his dear son George again. George was the youngest and probably his favorite.

Uncle Lars loved having his feet tickled so much that he would pay his sons if they would tickle his feet. He was such a successful farmer that he eventually bought a large and beautiful farm on what was called "the bottomland," which was much preferable to the hill farm that he moved from. Aunt Julia died some years before he moved. I've been told that her death was the result of her not taking insulin for her diabetes as directed. Lars remarried, but his second wife also preceded him in death.

My parents' next move was to build a cabin in the woods called a *hytte i skøven* in Danish ("hut in the woods"). The dwelling was very sparse, but it was a big improvement over the cowshed. It was located near Branson Cemetery in Loveland Iowa, where they are now interred. My father often talked about the pride he felt the first evening they spent in their new home. He sat at the table saying, "I'm sitting at my own table in my own house with my feet planted firmly under my own table!"

Ragnhild, their second child, was born in the newly built cabin. It was at this time that my parents decided to return to Denmark. They had become discouraged by their many struggles. Their most difficult and stressful challenge occurred during the birth of Eva, their first child. Mom was in labor for thirty-six hours. As she struggled to deliver Eva, my father wept and cried out, "Did I bring you to this country only to die?" Despite her great pain, my mother cried out over and over again that she was going to live. The circumstances were so dire that the physician gave up trying to deliver the baby or to save my mother and simply left both of them to die. In desperation, my father was able to find another doctor, who attempted to save the dying woman with a baby hopelessly lodged in the birth canal. But miraculously after thirty-six hours in labor, my mother gave birth to Eva. Both survived the ordeal, but my mother suffered such serious injuries that the doctor chose not to perform any repairs. He did not expect her to live, but she survived the ordeal.

My mother's second pregnancy ended in a miscarriage, caused by a fall while she was carrying a load of wood in her apron to the kitchen stove. The fall resulted in bleeding, which she brought to my father's attention. He was not worried and told her that he needed to do some work in the fields and would return later to see how she was doing. My father's lack of concern left my mother believing that everything must be all right, and so nothing further was done.

My parents were very discouraged by their situation in Iowa. There was not enough land to grow crops, and my father's brick mason work was very slow because there was little demand for his skills. They hung on for several years hoping things would improve. But it became apparent that their dreams of success in America were not going to be realized. My parents thought that happiness could be found in their homeland. Their decision to return to Denmark was a very difficult one. Uncle Lars and his family were dear to my parents, and Lars often provided a helping hand when their need was dire.

As my parents prepared for their return to Denmark in the spring of 1908, the beauty of their little cabin was at its best, with the warming weather, the wildflowers blossoming, and the birds singing. It must have felt as if they were leaving a little piece of paradise as they prepared for their journey home, wondering whether their few possessions and savings could pay for the cost of the trip. They reminisced about the conditions under which they felt compelled to leave Denmark and the emotions that forced them away to seek the freedom to consummate their love for each other in America. The difficult experiences and challenges they endured during their years in America gave them a measure of maturity and wisdom. They returned to Denmark wondering whether they would be able to realize the dreams they held in their hearts.

My grandparents were overjoyed to see their daughter and her husband return home, bringing with them their two beautiful granddaughters, Eva and Ragnhild. Hugs and kisses were shared, and smiles shined through their tears. For the moment, all things seemed bright and hopeful, but finding an affordable place to live in Denmark was not easy. My dad made plans to farm and to supplement his income by using his brick mason skills. They moved to a small farm, where they looked forward to a new beginning. The farmhouse was Spartan, and my mother was disappointed with the low door frames, which required them to stoop down when they walked from room to room. Nevertheless, they were optimistic about their new life, being near family, and having a sense of hope for the future.

My grandmother was delighted with my sister Ragnhild, and my grandfather enjoyed walks on the seashore hand in hand with Eva. Eva remembered finding a piece of amber as they walked and the delight she felt as they returned to his workshop, where he worked as a silversmith. He placed a wooden apple box alongside him for Eva to stand on while he worked, so she could watch him carve the amber into a beautiful heart-shaped pendant, sculpting a cross on one side and an anchored cross on the other. Eva's oldest daughter, Mary Ann, wears that amber pendant to this day.

A year after their return to Denmark, my mother gave birth to my brother Holger in May 1909. They delighted in having their first son, but life was difficult as they stretched their few resources by doing their many day-to-day chores. Still, my father was delighted to be back in Denmark. Ragnhild remembered him singing as he returned from the mill where he brought the harvested wheat for grinding. She said his singing stopped when they later returned to America for the second time.

My father was a handsome man and had often enjoyed dancing in his younger years before he met my mother. My mother, on the other hand, never had an opportunity to learn how to dance. She described one particular incident when there was a neighborhood dance that my father was eager to attend. On this particular occasion, he left my mother home with the children. She agreed to this, but it left her feeling inadequate and discouraged. Shortly after he left, a couple who lived nearby visited my mother. When they learned that my father had gone to the dance, their hearts went out to my mother, and they insisted she join him while they watched the children. Despite feeling very unsure of herself and doubtful about what she was about to do, she mustered her courage and went off to the dance to join my father. As she approached the dance hall, she could hear the music and see through the windows the fun that everyone was having. Her insecurity made her want to turn around and run, but she overcame her fear and slowly opened the door, looking around to find my father, Chris. She could see that he took great pride and pleasure in showing his talent for dancing, performing all the right steps and following the rhythm of the music perfectly. He probably did not notice her standing by the door, and she could have left without being noticed, but she summoned the courage to go inside and find a seat. But even then, no one acknowledged her presence. Eventually, my father noticed her. Sadly, as their eyes met, a frown appeared on his face. She knew her presence embarrassed him. Apprehension turned to sadness and regret for having gone to the dance. When the dance was over, she knew she was in for a scolding by my father. And so he questioned her, demanding to know why she would even consider coming without knowing how to dance, emphasizing how much of an embarrassment she was to him.

As time went on, my mother's feelings of disappointment and discouragement with her life grew worse, and she came to believe that things might never change. Although she had returned to Denmark with thoughts of a nicer home and a better life, her hopes were not materializing. My brother Holger was nearly two years old, and my mother was pregnant with her fourth child. She knew her parents were very aware of how hard life was for her. Knowing this was unsettling and a blow to my mother's pride. She began sharing her sadness and her thoughts of returning to America with my father, but I believe she chose not to share the real reason. Although my dad loved being back in Denmark, he was increasingly concerned about my mother's constant sadness. She no longer showed the happiness she had felt when they first arrived back in Denmark. Most of my father's family still lived in Denmark. He had no ties to his selfish father, but he was close to other family members with whom he shared memorable times.

Anders Poulsen Andersen was my father's oldest brother. Anders had a very sizable family of twelve children, and my mother was able to hire his twelve-year-old daughter, Stena, to help with the chores. After Anders married his fiancée, Maria (aka, Hedevig Maria), they were able to buy a farm. The land had not yet been cultivated, but they were able to turn it into a productive and successful farm. For this accomplishment, they were honored with a monument, which still exists to this day. Two of their children—Niels, who married Stena (who was also Danish), and Ernest, who married Lillian—owned farms in Iowa. Niels and Stena had two sons and a daughter. Ernest and Lillian also had several children.

Niels Agdahl was my father's youngest brother. Niels and his wife, Eva, had two children—a son, Tage, and a daughter, Kirstine. During my husband Bill's and my first trip to Denmark, we were invited to dinner at Tage's and Eva's home in Copenhagen. Tage shared memories of my brother Holger and he being swung in a rug held by my father and his brother Niels. Tage made at least one trip to the United States and became acquainted with my brothers Holger and Harvey. He played a role in the Danish underground resistance during World War II. We also met Tage's sister, Kirstine. I first learned of her when I was quite young, after my family received a picture of her as a teenager. I remember realizing how far apart we were, but the picture gave me a vivid feeling about her. In particular, I admired her long beautiful braids.

Niels Agdahl became a highly successful banker and chose to change his name from Andersen to Agdahl. He owned a farm early after his marriage but soon sold it. My father's sister Thea married Peter Jensen, and they had two daughters. My cousin Kirstine recalled how much she and her brother, Tage, loved to visit them. Thea coddled them, and they loved her dearly.

Kirstine said that my mother and father were regarded as the "good aunt and uncle from the United States," and thus there was always

great joy when they received their letters from America. I believe Tage had two sons and a daughter. Kirstine had a college degree in physical education and married a successful farmer by the last name of Toft. They had three sons and a daughter: Jorgen, Kaj, Sven and Ingrid. Knowing the Tofts has been a great joy to me and my family. Jorgen, his wife, Sonja, and Ingrid have visited us in America on several occasions.

My mother's brothers—Elias, John, and Otto—came to the United States. Elias married Maggie, and they had three children: Arthur, Irene, and Bobby. Uncle John married Marie, who was Danish, and they had two daughters: Alice and Marilyn. Otto married Dorothy Petersen, and they had a son, Kenneth. Dorothy's first husband had died from the Spanish flu. All of these relatives lived within five miles of each other. The siblings of my mother who remained in Denmark were Ane Kirstine, Jens Christian, Marie, Herman Axel Fredrick, Gudmund, and Eva.

My mother's sister Eva was the same age as my sister Eva. I know they played together because I remember my sister Eva relating how she ruined what her young aunt thought was a compliment from my father. He told her that she looked like a dirty pig, which she interpreted as the Danish expression *ducty pige*, which in Danish means "smart girl." My sister Eva told her the disappointing news that he really meant *spagut gras*, or dirty pig.

My aunt Eva and her mother (my grandmother) became very close, to the exclusion of my grandfather, making my aunt very spoiled. Reportedly, her mother once gave her a quick slap on the ear, which Eva quickly returned in kind. My grandmother Hanna (aka, Johanne) was a difficult person to live with and, as she grew older, became crippled with arthritis. She was an unreasonable person much of the time and made life for my grandfather quite difficult. Eventually, my grandfather moved out and went to live with his son Herman and his wife, while Eva and her mother lived together by themselves. Johanne was born on November 16, 1858, and died on March 22, 1931, at the age of seventy-three. My mother was informed of her death by mail. She wept as she read the news. My father's response was, "Why are you crying? What did she ever do for you?" My father remembered the worst about Hanna, whereas her death tugged at my mother's heartstrings. She felt the sadness that only a daughter could feel.

My grandfather Christensen was born on May 12, 1857, and died on October 10, 1937, when he was eighty years old. My cousin Greta Sorenson was a granddaughter of my uncle Chris in Denmark. Frode was a son of my uncle Chris. Frode remembered that my grandmother Hanna never visited Chris and that he never visited her. Frode remembered his grandfather visiting his parents, Chris and Marie, often. When he was a teenager, Frode frequently visited his grandfather while he was in his workshop. He and his friends brought scrap metal to sell to him. The story goes that the scrap metal was often collected by my grandfather himself and that he probably knew what they were bringing, but Frode and his friends still received payment for bringing my grandfather his own metal. In an old newspaper, Greta found a description of my grandfather Peter Gertler's (Christensen) funeral, telling of the many flowers at the service. He was remembered as a rescuer of sailors, using Lønstrup's lifeboats. They thanked the old man for his loyal and persistent work as a rescuer. The priest said that Peter was happy and aware of his coming death. He was filled with harmony and calm. This story reminds me of my mother's stories about taking lunch to him at the shore as he worked to rescue stranded ships. She loved being able to bring his lunch and spending time with him. She loved the ocean and enjoyed saying that she was part of the northern Vikings. Had she been a man, she would have lived her life on the sea. Her brother Chris was a fisherman with his own boat. Chris helped rescue World War II fliers who were shot down by the Germans. He plucked the fliers out of the water and carried them to Sweden. I don't know how often this happened, but he told of one incident when he was returning from one of his rescue missions to Sweden and was confronted by a German patrol officer at the landing. The officer questioned Chris about where he had been. Chris answered, "Am I not allowed to take my boat out for a morning of fishing?"

I suspect that my mother eventually broke the news to my grandparents that my parents were making plans to return to America with their four children. My grandparents must have been devastated. They had believed the harmony that existed between them and their daughter's family would bring them joy for the rest of their lives. My mother was forgiven, and the relationship with my father became one of acceptance on both sides. My grandmother even begged my mother to leave Ragnhild with her in Denmark, saying that my mother had three other little ones, but hers were nearly all gone. Preparations were under way, and I believe there were times when my mother wept, questioning why returning to Denmark had not given them the answers they had hoped for. All of the struggles they had endured in America kept returning in her thoughts. They had had barely enough money to pay for their voyage back to Denmark. It had seemed like such a lifesaving decision when they returned to life in Denmark, free of the strife that had enveloped them in America. I believe there were times when my mother fell into disbelief when they contemplated returning to what could be another test of their souls. I know my father loved life in Denmark, but he failed to understand the suffering my mother was going through. My mother made up her mind that she wanted to be free from the judgments of others. She believed she could gain this freedom by going back to America.

The preparations for returning to America began. My brother Harvey was born, and so my parents' family now included four children. Harvey was six months old at the time of their departure. My uncle Elias (my mother's brother), who was twenty-one years old at the time, helped soften the sadness of my mother. Elias made plans to return to America with my parents. He brought his nineteen-year-old girlfriend, Anna Jensen, with him. The day came when it was time to say their good-byes. I know tears were shed and there was confusion and many emotions over why their time in Denmark did not work out. My mother said her final good-bye to her parents, knowing she would never see them again. She was stoic and disciplined when they said good-bye. I believe she kept her emotions to herself until she could express them away from her parents. My dad later expressed regret for not having shown affection by kissing his mother-in-law good-bye. He said he knew my grandmother was hoping he would make this gesture at their parting, but he confessed that he was not able to bring himself to show her any affection.

So now they were off and on their way. Any regrets or dreams about what might have been, had to be put away to allow their thoughts to turn to the future and the life that awaited them in America.

My mother packed with great care knowing that she had very limited space to take her belongings, and so she was able to bring only necessities. Harvey needed diapers. She knew that Holger, at two years old, would be the hardest to manage on the trip because of his great curiosity and tendency to wander from her side. Eva was seven and provided the only help she had. Ragnhild stayed by her side during the trip, but as expected, Holger wandered off, following the ship's custodian as he opened the portal to dump trash into the ocean. The custodian was shocked when he saw Holger next to him. The child was so close to the portal that he could have followed the garbage into the ocean. The custodian turned quickly, striking Holger. Speaking Danish, Holger demanded to know why the custodian had struck him.

Holger also discovered a way to get attention and to make it profitable. There was a roped-off section that separated the men from the women, which was required on the ship. Families were allowed to see each other at scheduled times during the day. They would gather at the ropes for a brief time when they were reunited. Holger went in front of the crowd and began doing a dance for all to see. The men were so entertained that they threw coins at him, which delighted Holger. Because of the separation of the men and the women, my mother was in charge of every aspect of caring for her children. Water was very limited, but my mother saved enough to rinse Harvey's diapers. She wrung them out and slept with them to make them dry more quickly.

Like so many other immigrants to America, my family arrived at Ellis Island in New York City on November 20, 1912. They faced the big challenge of waiting their turn to pass through the health exam. Everyone feared being turned back because of being diagnosed with an unexpected illness. My mother was very unsure of herself. When she finally saw my father, she breathed a sigh of relief. However, once they passed the inspection, a whole new set of problems confronted them. Neither of them could speak English well enough to feel confident asking the questions they needed to raise. They felt swept away by the crowds and the fast pace of the world around them. They knew they needed to find the train that would take them to Iowa, but they barely knew where to start to solve this puzzle. Doubts flooded back into their minds, memories of their first trip to America returned, and for the moment, I think they panicked as they tried to push those memories away. My mother felt a heavy responsibility for leading her family back to what now loomed even larger in her mind. What would befall them this time? She must have breathed out a prayer in this new memory of what she had left in desperation, hoping Denmark would offer the solace and answers she sought. Determination was her only answer. She must have told herself that there would be no turning back this time. It would be up to her to make it work.

They found the train station, holding Holger tightly and carrying Harvey, while holding the hands of Eva and Ragnhild. They tried to avoid showing the frightened glances on their faces. I believe that when they arrived in Missouri Valley, Iowa, Uncle Lars was there to meet them and rescue them, while they wondered where they would go from there. Although my father was a brick mason, he knew this job alone would not sustain them. His hope was to buy a farm. I don't know the details of how he searched for a home, but I do know that he wanted to find something as soon as possible near Missouri Valley. I am also uncertain about where they lived during their first year back in America. I do know that life was a struggle, but a year later they moved onto the farm where their next six children would be born.

The farm they found was located five miles from Missouri Valley in what was called the hilly area. My dad borrowed the money for the first payment on the mortgage from Aunt Julia's father. The farm had a very large ditch that ran through the property as well as a wooded area of considerable size. The crops would have to be planted on the hilly ground. Unfortunately, the challenge this represented was not apparent to my father. When they moved into their home, there were barely enough beds to accommodate them. I cannot imagine how their needs were met, but they likely felt great relief having found a place to live.

The weather was very cold. They had a large wood cooking stove in the kitchen that provided heat as they hovered around it. Cutting trees and chopping wood for fuel was one of their big challenges. There were trees in the woods nearby, but it was a nearly impossible task to cut the trees to the size they needed, since they had only a hand saw. The furnace that provided heat in the room next to the kitchen likewise required wood for fuel.

Every minute counted in providing warmth and food. As Christmas approached, my mother racked her brain thinking of what gifts she could find to surprise the children. She probably bought an orange for each stocking and a few pieces of hard candy. She probably held back her tears in disappointment. My father cut a small tree in the woods, which added a fragrance to their home that became part of their memories. My mother undoubtedly prepared chicken in her best way with potatoes and gravy. After finishing dinner, they stood near the tree and sang Christmas carols. Then a sudden knock at the door brought the singing to a halt. My father went to the door and cautiously opened it, while Eva, Ragnhild, and Holger looked on in astonishment. There in the doorway stood someone dressed as Santa Claus with a pack on his back and shouting "Merry Christmas!" The surprise was beyond their imaginations. Santa set down his bag and began handing out presents. I believe my mother was giddy with joy. There were presents for everyone and probably Christmas candy as well. After hugging everyone in my family, Santa once more shouted "Merry Christmas" as he opened the door and disappeared into the darkness, with Eva, Ragnhild, and Holger's eyes following him. My father closed the door as everyone yelled their good-byes to Santa. The cold from the outside went unnoticed as they jumped and screamed in delight and opened the gifts, holding each one close to their hearts.

It was not until the following day that they learned who this wonderful Santa Claus was. He was a neighbor, Mr. Kirkland, who was aware of my Danish family's move to the property, which was next to his own. He and his wife, in their caring thoughts, surmised the hardships my family were facing and transformed their otherwise lonely Christmas Eve into a joy that would be forever remembered.

This new life in America became a shocking reality to my family. When they gave up and decided to return to Denmark after their first journey to America, they had only two children. The harsh reality that they didn't have the same options they had before dawned on them. I am certain they looked around and wondered about the likelihood of survival. They were in the dead of winter, they were struggling to keep warm, and they were confronting the thought of how they would get through this monumental challenge. I believe my mother cried many nights, but she knew that their survival was up to her. She was the family's leader. Her dear friend Aunt Carey, who was married to my father's cousin Andrew, opened her heart to my mother's needs. Aunt Carey had clothing her children had worn that she was able to hand down to my mother. My sister Ragnhild said she heard my mother's treadle sewing machine working into the night as my mother remade the clothes to fit her children. Eva, who was seven years old, was sent to school as soon as possible. She went to Bennett School, a one-room schoolhouse where grades one through eight were taught. Eva paved the way for Ragnhild, Holger, and Harvey. She knew little or no English, but she mustered the courage to endure the ridicule and laughter from her classmates hearing her speak her "funny" language. She walked a mile and a half to and from school through deep snow and bad weather. Her odd clothes were necessary to protect her from the unbearable cold.

Slowly, my parents accumulated sufficient furniture so that their house began to feel a little more like a home. My parents were connected to a series of families via the telephone line. This gave them a measure of security that they had never before realized. They purchased a couple of horses and a buggy, so they could now travel to the town of Missouri Valley for groceries and other supplies. My mother made wool quilts from the scraps left over from the clothes she remade. She also knew how to make slippers for the family by stitching together many pieces of fabric that served as soles for their slippers; then she cut the top to fit over the sole and carefully sewed it in place. The slippers were very warm and served as indoor shoes. Trying to find a way to feed the family was the greatest challenge of all. That first winter, my mother was unable to grow a garden and prepare canned fruits and vegetables as she would be able to do in the future. I suspect someone gave them an animal to butcher, which she used to can meat. Aunt Carey and Uncle Lars and Aunt Julia probably gave her canned fruits and vegetables to get them through the winter. Their kind neighbors the Kirklands probably shared food with them as well.

When I reflect on my parents' situation, I am amazed to think that they would bring their four children to a state of questionable survival. When spring finally arrived, the farm showed hope with wildflowers in bloom and singing birds nesting in the blossoming trees. But spring also meant that every thought had to be directed toward planting the fields and the garden. Neither of my parents had experience running a farm. Uncle Lars helped my father by providing insights into farming, but my dad questioned how he would be able to support his family. He hoped he would be able to use his talents as a brick mason to get them through.

My dad remembered the days in Denmark when he had herded cattle. He still believed, as he did then, that cattle could be managed without the use of fences. Eva and Ragnhild were put to work pulling weeds. Ragnhild was five years old when spring arrived, and Eva had turned eight in September. When Dad told them if they didn't pull weeds they would go to the poorhouse, Ragnhild started crying while she pulled weeds. She told Eva she was afraid they would go to the poorhouse. Eva answered her, "You are so silly! The poorhouse couldn't be any worse than this."

My father was trying to adjust to the ways of farming, but it was not easy. The hilly terrain made planting and harvesting very difficult, and my father liked shortcuts and simplicity. Of course, the truth was that there were no easy ways for him to learn how to farm. Uncle Lars was doing well, but it had taken him years to learn to be a successful farmer, and the learning process was a resounding challenge. Years later, when my father was relying on his brick mason skills for income, he stated, "I'm a dollar-an-hour man, not a farmer." As soon as the children were able, they took their places doing chores. Eva was the first child to be initiated into doing chores, because she was the oldest. She continued helping both of my parents for years. Holger was the oldest of the boys and therefore was the first of the sons to take responsibility performing chores. My mother planted a garden as early as the weather allowed and canned beans, carrots, tomatoes, and pears.

She saved her pennies so she could buy apples, plums, and peaches, which she canned as well. As soon as the pigs were large enough, one was butchered, and her job was to cut the bones and pieces of meat small enough for canning. This allowed them to have meat over the winter. Now she had chickens to supply the family with eggs, and the baby chicks soon grew large enough for her to clean and sell at the local stores, which provided grocery money.

Holger was seven years old when he was sent to the field to repair a barbed-wire fence that needed a staple replaced. While he was attempting to repair the fence, the staple he was pounding to the post flew off and hit him in his right eye. He panicked and ran home screaming for help. My mother was beside herself with panic and grief. Holger was rushed to see Dr. Tamisea, who was an alcoholic and had been drinking when he examined Holger's eye. The doctor began squeezing Holger's eye, causing liquid to flow from the wound. My parents were left feeling even more devastated. The next morning, his eye was very red and swollen. My parents then sought the help of Dr. Heise, whom they had seen before. For reasons unknown, they had not taken Holger to him the previous night. Dr. Heise was astounded with what he saw and exclaimed there was nothing he could do. The only hope was for Holger to go to the Gifford Clinic in Omaha. My father drove Holger to Omaha, possibly by horse and buggy. After he was examined, my father was told Holger's right eye was in critical condition and the vision in his left eye was also threatened. Both of Holger's eyes were bandaged. Although my father visited him every day, time passed slowly for Holger. In his desperation, he thought two days had passed instead of only one. Despite his condition, he told my father it was all right that he did not come to see him as he said he would, even though he actually did see him. Holger remained at the clinic for several days, not knowing his outcome. When the bandages were finally removed, they realized he was blind in his right eye. My brother Harold, who was the next child born after Holger, recalled that when they were older and hunted together, Holger always aimed the rifle from his left eye.

The tragedy of Holger's loss of vision in his right eye followed the family for many years. It caused my mother great sadness as she thought about what this accident would do to Holger's life and his future. He and my mother were very close, and she cultivated his intense curiosity when she cleaned and prepared chickens. Holger often watched her work, and she noticed how interested he was in the chicken's organs, like the heart. He would cut open the heart, trying to understand how it worked. She told him he had the hands of a surgeon. I believe my father was pained by Holger's injury, but he suffered in a different way than my mother. He may have harbored some guilt, but my dad sought perfection in everything, and Holger's disability seemed to be a problem for my dad. There was also an element of jealousy. My father wanted Holger to be strong and accept all of the responsibilities he would have to assume. As Holger grew older, there was obvious friction and arguing between them. My mother remembered that at times they chose not to be in the house at the same time. Each of them would knock at the back door to check whether the other one was in the house. If one of them was, the other would choose to stay outside.

Harold was born on September 12, 1913. My parents now had five children and therefore more responsibilities. Eva was Dad's main helper, and she also became the second mother to her siblings. She was often more of a disciplinarian than my mother was. Ragnhild, being three years younger than Eva, worked under her guidance.

By this time, my dad was becoming more adept at farming. He worked long hours and ate his dinner well after the sun was down. My brothers feared his strong reprimands if they did not accomplish the work they were assigned to do. Holger started attending Bennett School after Eva and Ragnhild had spent time there. They felt somewhat secure in school. Holger was very sensitive and did not feel accepted by the older boys. This was another hardship he had to face. One of the older farmhands who still attended school was a bully and pegged Holger for a sissy, and his cruelty followed. Holger was made to eat dog manure. He was pushed around and teased. The abuse continued for about two years until the bully finally graduated from the eighth grade. Eventually, all ten Andersen children graduated from the eighth grade at Bennett School. Each of us had different experiences, but none of us escaped the insecurities of feeling like foreigners, Danes trying to adjust to whatever was expected of us. We continued to speak Danish at home until we graduated from high school, when we left home. We all felt we were in a foreign land living in an alien society. Without Eva's help, my mother could not have managed. She worked side by side with my mother.

Esther was born on November 15, 1915. Three of her brothers were born before Esther, who was followed by three more brothers. Esther had only her brothers who were there for her. Because my mother was so busy, she had little loving contact with Esther. At one time, Esther told me she wanted a hug from my mother so badly, she asked my mother if she ever felt like running into the arms of her mother. This wasn't a question my mother wanted to deal with, having so many other children and chores that needed attention. In frustration, she responded to Esther by saying, "Is that how you feel?" When Esther responded that she did in fact feel that way, my mother responded tersely, "Then why don't you do it?"

Ken was born in December 1924. Esther became Ken's second mother. She assumed responsibility for most of Ken's needs, beginning when he was just a few months old. She was so devoted to Ken that she became extremely lonesome while she visited my sister Eva and her husband, Harold. She desperately wanted to make sure that Ken was all right. Since she had no sisters close to her age, she joined her brothers in their escapades. She learned early on to defend herself. She was very close to her older brother Holger, who advised her to "learn to dance, and date many men to make a good choice in the man you marry. Don't be like your two older sisters, Eva and Ragnhild, who married the first guys who came along." Esther followed his advice.

In many ways, Esther was like her brother Harold, in that she loved to dance and party. I remember the two of them dancing to Victrola records, and both of them danced with me by the time I was ten years old when they needed a fill-in. Esther was Ken's and my biggest advocate. I remember an incident when Harold pushed me away from him because I had pinkeye. Esther threw a bucket of soapy water used for washing the floor onto his chicken pox sores. Harold would have attacked Esther, but my dad arrived just in time to save her.

Esther left for high school when she was thirteen years old. She worked for her room and board for two years for Eva and Howard (Eva's second husband), and the next two years she worked for an acquaintance of Eva's, Gertrude Brown. After graduation from high school, she started nurses training in Council Bluffs at the Jenny Edmundson Hospital. She loved nursing and was a very conscientious nurse.

Since our family lived five miles from Missouri Valley and we were therefore a long way from high school, my parents allowed Holger, Eva, and Ragnhild to stay in an apartment in Missouri Valley for a short while. I think Harvey and the other boys had to walk the five miles to school. My brother Chris, the eighth of the ten children, born January 26, 1920, lived with our brother Harvey and Harvey's wife, Wilma, in Omaha during his last two years of high school, but he walked to school with Henry during his first two years.

Holger gave Ken a bicycle for transportation to and from high school. Unfortunately, it did not work out well, because the snowy winters and the wet springs made bike riding impossible. As a result, he stayed with Eva part of the time and the rest of the time with Henry and Stella. By his junior year, one of the students from a nearby farm drove a car and picked up Ken at the end of our lane.

Eva was the first of the ten children to graduate from grade school. She was reluctant to leave my father without her help and thus did not want to go on to high school. Ragnhild finished grade school three years after Eva and was eager to start high school. After a year of observing Ragnhild's enthusiasm for school, Eva started high school the following fall. She was able to finish in only three years by concentrating on her course work. They both took classes that allowed them to teach grade school following graduation. Ragnhild was successful at teaching, but Eva was not able to control some of her students and, as a result, was not rehired. It was at this time that my dad told Eva she should consider marrying Harold Jensen so that people would assume her marriage was the reason she left teaching.

A home wedding was planned for Eva in December 1925 when she was 21 years old. Ken was barely one year old. My mother had eight children still at home, ranging in age from one to eighteen years. Ragnhild was teaching and had an interest in Ted, who was Harold Jensen's first cousin. The wedding was as fine as my mother could arrange with all of her other responsibilities. Eva and Harold moved to a farm in Moorhead and began a joyous life together. Shortly afterward Ragnhild and Ted eloped, in July 1926. Ted's father gave them a farm, also in Moorhead. Eva and Ragnhild were very happy to be living so close to each other.

My mother, who was in declining health, told me that Ragnhild saw the possibility of her mother's death and realized what lay ahead in her future if she, being the oldest, was chosen to care for the entire family. Ted and Ragnhild eloped a month after Eva's marriage. Eva and Harold planned a picnic with Ted and Ragnhild and other friends. It was a warm Iowa afternoon, and they were all eager to enjoy a day of fun at the nearby river. Harold in particular loved the water and swimming. He was the only one who knew how to swim, and so he came prepared, dressed in his swimsuit. After some jokes and laughter, Harold, not wanting to lose any more time out of the water, made a long run and jumped in, calling back, "I'm going to swim the river of Jordan!" He hadn't gone far when the others heard his shouting for help. No one else knew how to swim, and so they stood helplessly—except for Eva, who was five months pregnant. Wanting to jump into the river to rescue Harold, she fought to pull away from those who were holding her back. She screamed to her husband but could only watch in despair.

Eva came home to stay with my parents after Harold drowned and was now living in a house with seven siblings. My mother comforted Eva and planned with her the joy their two babies would have together. My mother was three months pregnant with me, the last of her ten children.

Part 2

My Siblings

Part 2 presents the recollections of me and my nine siblings growing up in a family of ten children, reflecting on their personalities and how they related to my parents and to each other. I hope these accounts will be woven into the fabric of the Andersen family, making it a more colorful and complete story. I leave it to the reader to decide how the Andersen children's lives were shaped by circumstances within my family and the larger external events that affected so many people who lived during the Great Depression and World War II.

Eva Kirstine

Eva's and Ragnhild's husbands were from Moorhead, Iowa. They were Danish and also were cousins. Eva and Ragnhild were three years apart instead of the two years separating most of the Andersen children. This is because my mother had a miscarriage between their births as the result of a fall. Eva was my mother's best friend from the time she was old enough to recognize her. I believe Eva provided a great deal of the understanding my mother needed but did not get from my father. From the very beginning, Eva was a strength in sharing in the care of her siblings. Esther remembered that Ragnhild and the others under Eva's control rebelled one day, ganging up on Eva. My mother gave Eva full control and support in her role as second mother. Eva had a very sweet spirit and a tenderness toward my father that strengthened his dependence on her as the oldest child. Although fully intending to go to high school, she stayed home to help my mother and father. After Ragnhild started high school, Eva resumed her education and finished high school in three years instead of four.

Eva was a very calm person and worried less about life than Ragnhild did. As I mentioned in part 1, shortly after moving to our farm, Dad told them that if they did not pull weeds, they would go to the poorhouse. Ragnhild became depressed because pulling weeds seemed like a never-ending chore. She expressed her dismay to Eva about going to the poorhouse. Eva responded to Ragnhild by saying, "Silly, could the poorhouse be any worse than this?" Eva and Ragnhild shared responsibilities during these early years in their life on the farm. They served as mothers to the younger children and learned to be responsible at an early age. As I said in part 1, as time went on, Eva, Ragnhild, and Holger were able to spend some of their time in an apartment in Missouri Valley during their high school years. My dad was especially proud of Eva and Ragnhild and presented them with gold watches when they graduated from high school. Their training curriculum in high school allowed them to teach country school, which they both did before marriage. Their pay was at most about forty dollars a month. The money paid for their own room and board, and they were also janitors and furnace stokers. Eva's teaching job did not last long, because of her inability to control the students, and my father advised Eva to get married so that people would not discover the reason her teaching job was terminated. She and Harold moved to a farm in Moorhead, Iowa and began a joyous life together.

As was described in part 1, Eva and Harold attended a picnic on a hot August day in 1926. Ragnhild and her husband, Ted, were part of the group celebrating the pleasant summer day. Harold was eager to get into the cool river and dove in saying, "I'm going to swim the river of Jordan." He swam out some distance, and then it became apparent he needed help. No one else knew how to swim, and during the ensuing panic, Eva had to be restrained from jumping into the river to rescue him. She was six months pregnant. Unfortunately, Harold drowned, leaving Eva devastated. She returned home to be with my parents, and three months later, she gave birth to a nine-pound girl she named Haroldine. It is believed that Haroldine was infected by a visitor who used her handkerchief to wipe a tear from Haroldine's eye causing a fatal Erysipelas infection. As Haroldine suffered, she could be heard sighing in pain. Eva held her and rocked her the entire night before she died, on December 11, 1926. My mother had a dream that night in which she heard a knock at the door. She opened the door and saw Harold standing there. When my mother asked him why he was there, he answered, "I've come for my little girl." Eva was heartbroken and relied on my parents for strength. She said that embroidering helped her as she worked through her grief. My mother was pregnant with me during this crisis, and I was born on February 3, 1927, less than two months after Haroldine died.

Eva took responsibility for the care of the family while my mother left to give birth to me in Missouri Valley at Aunt Carey's home. Ken had whooping cough during this time. My mother returned home about two weeks later and kept me isolated from the others in the house. Eva lived at home for two years but eventually realized that she had to make other plans. Unfortunately, any decision to change her situation was not likely to offer her the security she was so desperate to have. She chose to go to work for a widower named Howard Nelson, whose wife had died, leaving him with two girls, LaVonne and Ardelle, ages two and four. Howard was a very cold and unattached man. Eva worked for Howard for one year. Then the inevitable happened, and she married Howard. On the day of the marriage, Howard took off enough time from work to drive with Eva to Omaha, where they were married by the justice of the peace. Following the ceremony, he dropped her off at their house and returned to work running a pool hall that he owned. He also managed a diner called the Soda Grill. Eva was expected to bake pies for the Soda Grill. He would come home from his work at around three in the morning and demanded strict quiet while he slept. He then returned to work at around noon. He treated Eva like a child who had to fulfill his every demand. She soon lost all confidence in herself and abided strictly by his rules.

Eva became pregnant shortly after their marriage. During this time, she was not allowed to mention the fact that she was pregnant. Many years later, a grandson who was pursuing his family history discovered that Howard's first wife had died from a self-induced abortion.

When Eva delivered her baby, the doctor used a medication to speed her dilation. The baby girl was fully developed but was born dead. In her grief, Eva prepared the clothes that her baby, Barbara, was to wear for her burial. Eva's next child, Mary Ann, was born on August 8, 1932, and was a great joy for Eva. Mary Ann was eager to please her parents and showed very adult-like behavior. Her father admired her and expected her to make him proud in everything she did. At a young age, he brought her to the city jail and left her inside momentarily so that she would know what to expect if she ever followed certain ways of the world, such as smoking or using nail polish.

Howard Allen was born on November 1, 1933. His father criticized him harshly, and therefore Howard Allen had low self-esteem and little confidence. Their next child, Carolyn, was born on September 22, 1935. She was a spunky girl and tried to defend herself, but very early on she became a victim of Howard's cruelty. She would hold her blanket with an edge in her mouth but her father warned her that this was unacceptable. He returned home early one morning and found the blanket in her mouth again. As punishment, he brought her outside, mashed tomato worms and smeared them on her blanket, and then shoved the blanket into her mouth. Their son Jim was born on September 9, 1942. He escaped much of Howard's cruelty by trying hard to follow his father's wishes.

After the children left and Howard retired, Eva became morose and depressed. Over the years that followed, she complained of intestinal pain, which could not be diagnosed. She was given pain medication, but it did not help. She and Howard moved to a retirement home where Eva continued to be in great pain. Following her death, my brother Ken, who had become a physician, eventually figured out that the constant pain was due to celiac access syndrome (abdominal pain caused by compression of a large blood vessel called the celiac artery). Eva died on January 8, 1994, in an assisted-living facility, where she lived her last years with Alzheimer's disease that was discovered following an autopsy. Howard had died several years before Eva did. The last time I visited Eva, Howard called Eva a "bad girl" because she begged for pain medication.

Eva was my mother's closest friend, but during my mother's last days living in her own house, they were no longer able to have the same helpful conversations they had had in the past, because Eva was bedridden and frail. Howard chastised my mother when she would try to call Eva, since she (Eva) was a "sick woman." When my mother was moved to a nursing home near my brother Holger in Strawberry Point, Iowa, she continued to talk about Eva and requested her presence more than anyone else's. Holger's wife, Viola, came to see my mother daily and reported my mom's desire to see Eva.

Ragnhild Alma

My mother used to point out the contrasts between Eva and Ragnhild from the time they were small children. Ragnhild was beautiful, and my mother received many compliments about her beauty. But my mother would say, "If you were raising her, you wouldn't find her so attractive." Ragnhild was a very sensitive and bright child who seemed to carry the weight of the world on her shoulders. Eva would often give up things for Ragnhild in order to please my mother and to reduce conflicts. Ragnhild remembered a great deal about her life during the short time the family lived in Denmark (she was the only sibling in the family who retained the ability to read Danish). She recalled my dad singing when he walked through the door at night, coming home from work, but the singing ceased after their return to America. She vividly remembered my dad saving Grandma Christensen from choking by grabbing her and turning her upside down while pounding on her back. Ragnhild was filled with awe for his having saved her grandmother's life. My grandma loved Ragnhild so much, she begged my parents to let her stay in Denmark when they decided to return to America. I believe Ragnhild and Eva graduated from high school the same year, since Eva had delayed starting high school to help on the farm. Both Eva and Ragnhild shared an interest in becoming teachers.

Eva and Ragnhild were dating their future spouses at the same time. Both men resided in Moorhead and were cousins. When Eva married Harold Jensen in 1925, Ragnhild was the oldest unmarried daughter in the family. This made it likely that Ragnhild would have to step in to care for the family if my mother were to die. It was my mother's belief that Ragnhild's decision to marry Ted at that time was influenced by this fear. Thus Ragnhild married Ted Johnson in July 1926. They inherited Ted's parents' farm in Moorhead. The house was attractive, and the farm was nicer than our family farm, with fewer hills and no ditch. The buildings were also in better shape. However, as was the case with our farm, there were no electric lights, faucets, or toilets inside.

Ragnhild was very lonesome and depressed. She told me she tried to think of positive things to make getting up in the morning easier. After each child was born, Ragnhild needed one of her sisters to be there to help her deal with her depression. Her first child, Richard, was born nine months after I was. I remember that we enjoyed his visits during the summer. He drew cartoons on long rolls of paper, which we attached to spindles, providing entertainment for my parents and siblings as we unrolled them. My brother Ken provided sound effects of gunshots by using a hammer to strike the head of a match placed on the bottom of Mother's clothes irons. (The irons were placed on the cooking stove until they became hot, and then were alternated as they cooled).

Ragnhild did not get to see us often. Although we lived only thirty miles apart, traveling that distance took much more time due to limited transportation and poor roads. She was not able to talk often to my mother because of the expensive long-distance telephone charges. I think Ragnhild liked having her family visit her, and I always enjoyed going there as a child. I loved hearing the rooster crow in the morning, which I never heard on our farm. I can remember driving to see them one winter in our Model A Ford. In order to keep warm, my mother heated bricks that we held close to our feet during the long, cold trip.

Ragnhild always seemed to talk fast and tended to stoop when standing. She was not one to show her affection easily, though she was conscientious in remembering birthdays and special events. She often did Holger's laundry, which she requested he send to her periodically in order to help Mom, who usually did this chore. This work included ironing many of his shirts. I remember the wonderful divinity candy she sent my dad on his birthday; I would sneak a taste after I picked up the mail on my way home from school and discovered my dad's birthday gift of the candy.

Ragnhild seemed to need more help from my family compared with my other married siblings. If her husband, Ted, was incapacitated even for a short time, she called for help, and the family usually responded to her needs. Eva's daughters, Mary Ann and Carolyn, have fond memories of their summer vacations with Ragnhild. Ragnhild enjoyed them a great deal, and she was a salvation for Mary Ann, who said she dreaded going home so much that she hid when her parents came to retrieve her. She feels that Ragnhild emotionally saved her life. Ragnhild's daughter Joyce was born on November 24, 1935, and Sharon followed on March 13, 1939. When Sharon was in high school, Ragnhild went back to teaching country school, and my mother, who had lost my father by then, kept house for Ted during the week. The weekly pay from Ragnhild allowed my mother to collect a Social Security pension of thirty-nine dollars per month.

Ragnhild and Ted sold their farm when Ragnhild was sixty-five, and they moved in with my eighty-five-year-old mother in Missouri Valley. This arrangement didn't work out as well as they had hoped. I suspect that my mother lost her feeling of independence. After two years, she became ill and went to stay with Esther. Six to nine months later, my mother went to a nursing home in Strawberry Point, Iowa, where Holger was the attending physician. My mother loved his daily visits. She was a very agreeable patient. She often commented on how good they were to her and said that she should be helping them. My mother died on May 13, 1974, having been a widow since 1951. Ragnhild and Ted moved to a retirement center in Missouri Valley several years after my mother's death.

Ted died several years before Ragnhild did. Soon after his death, Ragnhild went to live with her daughter Sharon for a short time, but then she moved to Everett, Washington, for two years to live with Richard and his wife, Joanne. Finally, she moved to Logan, Iowa, when Richard's declining health made it difficult for her to live with them. Ragnhild died in a nursing home several years later, on September 9, 1993. I remember visiting her on a trip home to Iowa, where I stayed with Henry's wife, Stella, in Logan. I was able to visit with her for several days. She was very appreciative of my visits and commented that she never really got to know me. I felt she was expressing her fondness for me and seemed to wish we had been closer. She also asked me if she was ugly. I answered, "Of course not!" Ragnhild was possibly the most beautiful of all four sisters. Through the years, I believe her continuously fearful nature likely contributed to her poor health.

Holger Martin

Holger was born in Denmark on May 19, 1909, during the few years that my parents lived in Denmark before returning to the United States. His Danish birth and roots gave him considerable pride. As a child, he was curious about everything. As I mentioned in part 1, while the family was on the ship headed for America, as Holger wandered around, he nearly fell out of a portal used for dumping garbage into the ocean. He was grabbed just in time by one of the ship's workers as the garbage was being dumped. Unaware of the danger, Holger asked if the worker was trying to hit him as he thrust his hands in front of Holger, saving him from falling and certain death.

Coming back to America posed a number of trials for Holger. He was a thin, delicate boy and enough of a worrier that he became a target of one of the senior farmhands, who was still attending Bennett School. Holger was tied to a post with a fire lit near him. Dog feces was shoved into his mouth during the taunts and teasing. Even more humiliating, Holger had to wear girls' lace boots with heels, since that was all my mother had from the hand-me-downs that fit him. Holger said he begged and cried and would gladly have gone in his bare feet instead of wearing girls' lace boots.

Since my dad needed all the help he could get on the newly purchased farm, he recruited Holger, who was seven years old. As was mentioned in part 1, Holger was sent into the field to mend some barbed wire that had come loose from the staples holding it in place on the fence posts. While Holger was hammering a staple, it flew into the air, striking him in the eye. For some reason, my parents did not take Holger to our usual doctor, and the doctor who initially treated him had been drinking, and with dirty hands, he squeezed Holger's eye, causing liquid to flow from it. The following day, my parents brought him to Dr. Heise, who wouldn't touch the eye because it looked infected. Dr. Heise sent Holger to a specialist named Dr. Gifford in Omaha. Holger was hospitalized with bandages on both eyes. Time seemed to pass very slowly; one day felt like two. Holger said he thought Dad changed his mind about coming to visit him yesterday as he had said he would. When the bandages were removed and Holger left the hospital, he was blind in his right eye, which took on a dull, cloudy cast.

Dad and Holger did not get along well. My mother said if one of them was inside, the other would stay outside after asking where the other one was. My mother remembered when Holger arrived home from high school, driving the horse and buggy. He was very cold as he entered the house, not answering Dad as he ordered him to unhitch the horse first. My father shouted, "Are you not only blind but deaf?" Hearing this, my mother wept in sadness for Holger. I have often wondered whether my dad felt guilty about Holger's eye injury and Holger's presence exacerbated that guilt. My mother encouraged Holger's interest in medicine by showing him the chambers in chicken hearts as she prepared chicken for dinner. As he examined the chicken parts, she told him he had the hands of a surgeon.

Holger graduated from high school in 1926 and worked as a farm laborer and section hand for two years in order to earn enough money for college. In 1928, he started at Morningside College in Sioux City, Iowa. In his second year, he transferred to the University of Iowa and pursued premedical training. In 1930, he started medical school, and he graduated with his medical degree in 1934. During his medical school training, Holger removed a piece of glass that was lodged in my finger. He later told my mom he regretted being so stern with me, cutting out the glass without using any pain medication. He used to scare me when he followed me with his stethoscope. I was afraid of what he might diagnose and what he would do to me as a result.

The Great Depression was a continuing source of obstacles and worries despite Holger's determination to achieve his goals. During his first summer at college, he stayed on campus doing odd jobs at thirty-five cents an hour. During this time, the Johnson County Savings Bank went broke, and Holger lost his entire tuition savings. When the college dean learned that Holger was being forced to withdraw from college due to lack of money, he arranged a personal loan of forty dollars for Holger. Additional financial help came from a scholarship fund, and dormitory housing became available in a converted high school gym for one dollar per month. During one particularly difficult time, Holger's food consisted of a bushel of apples that supplied him for at least a week. When he worked in the college cafeteria, he chose a wage instead of food. His food came from the scraps left in the kettles he washed.

Holger had to hitchhike home wearing shoes with soles worn through and cardboard inserts in them. He sent his laundry home in a heavy khaki mailer for my mother to wash. Sometimes Ragnhild volunteered to do Holger's laundry. The postage was twenty-five cents. On one occasion, my mother didn't have any money to return his washed laundry. In desperation, she went to the basement to see if any money might have fallen from the grates above to the furnace housing below. She was thrilled when she found the twenty-five cents she needed. Another difficulty was having to use heavy cast-iron plates that my mother heated on the cookstove to do her ironing.

Holger did his internship at the Epworth Hospital in South Bend, Indiana. In one of his notable stories, thirty minutes after he started his rotation in the emergency room, ambulances brought sixteen victims from a shoot-out with the infamous criminal John Dillinger that took place during a bank robbery. Four people were dead on arrival, two or three others had minor injuries, and six to eight people were admitted to the hospital. In 1936, Holger began his practice in the town of Strawberry Point, Iowa. The town of 3,500 people had only two physicians when Holger arrived. He married Viola Watts on December 24, 1936. Holger had met her through my sister Esther, who was with Viola in nurses' training. Holger and Viola had two children—Jon Allen, born on March 13, 1938, and Jane, born on September 20, 1941.

During Holger's early practice, house calls and home births were common. Holger's wife, Viola, assisted him on many of his house calls. She provided the gauze mask for anesthesia while he delivered the babies. Some of the most gratifying experiences of Holger's career were the more than three thousand deliveries he performed, for as many as four generations of his patients. He said that the biggest medical breakthroughs during his medical career were the discovery of penicillin and other antibiotics, as well as the polio vaccine. He was an outstanding physician and was known for his exceptional diagnostic abilities, so he was often consulted by other physicians. From very early in his practice, he successfully delivered breech babies. He delivered his first breech birth during a house call, even though he had only read about the technique. Nevertheless, he successfully accomplished the delivery.

America was at war with Germany in 1941. Holger felt an allegiance to his adopted country and chose to enlist in the armed forces as a physician in the medical corps in 1942. Holger and his wife, and their two children, Jon and Jane, were sent to Camp Crowder in Joplin, Missouri. One of his most vivid memories of his time at Camp Crowder was of the troops being sent on practice missions with minimal water, often to the point that they would pass out. Taking matters into his own hands, Holger sent a complaint directly to the commanding general, bypassing the usual chain of command. The general was furious with Holger for his audacity in not following normal protocol, and he responded with an intimidating reprimand. Ultimately, however, he was so impressed with Holger that he chose him as his personal physician. Later on, the general received orders to relocate overseas and requested that Holger accompany him. Holger was deemed unqualified, however, because he was blind in one eye. Holger subsequently learned that the general and his group were all killed in an ambush overseas. When Holger returned to Strawberry Point to resume practicing civilian medicine three and a half years later, he had to start his practice all over again.

I often suggested to Holger that he write about his unusual experiences as a physician. One experience which I remember was the time a man called Holger to report that his wife was hemorrhaging. Holger arrived at the house and examined the woman. He became convinced that she had just given birth and asked them where the baby was. The husband became angry and ordered Holger to leave. Holger then went to the police who returned with him to the house. This time the police insisted that they be told where the baby had been disposed. The man finally led Holger and the police to the outhouse where the baby had been dumped. The feces in the outhouse generated enough heat that the baby was still alive and thus survived.

Holger retired at age seventy. Upon his retirement, a celebration was held in his honor that thousands of people attended. The traffic in Strawberry Point was so congested that extra police had to be called on duty. Holger and Viola moved to Naples, Florida, in 1980 after he retired. He enjoyed the canal that passed by their home. He loved fishing from his front yard, and he no longer pursued an active social life. During the last few years of his life, he began to repeat his sentences and, on one occasion, was unable to discern whether he was home or visiting his brother Ken. During the six months before Holger died, he was very restless at night and wandered a lot of the time. He experienced pain in his chest the morning of his death on December 16, 1988. He went to the hospital following the pain but chose to return home. In the early afternoon as he sat at the table eating with Viola and one of his granddaughters, he suddenly called to Viola and then died at that moment.

My husband, Bill, and I visited Holger about a year before he died. As we waited at the airport on our way home, Holger shed tears, thinking that he would never see us again. I too became very sad realizing that my brother would not continue to be a part of our big family much longer. I could not imagine my family without Holger.

Harvey Arthur

Harvey always brought sunshine into my life. I remember that he was a peacemaker and he had a very positive attitude. My parents trusted him implicitly. He never complained to my parents, and I always felt that things would remain calm when he was around. My father trusted Harvey. When an important chore needed to be done, he would carefully explain it to Harvey, adding, "I know I can trust you." In contrast, he found it hard to trust or give credit to Harvey's younger brother Harold even when he deserved it. Although Harold's recollection of Harvey was that he did less work than his brothers, he still received high praise from his father.

Harvey was also very close to my mother. Later in life, during walks together with me along the beaches in Santa Cruz, California, he shared how as a child, he worried so much about her that he suffered fearful nightmares of her dying.

Harvey started attending the University of Iowa in 1930. He enjoyed making new social contacts, especially with the family he was fortunate to board with—a physician and his two children, whom Harvey chauffeured in the family car. It was difficult for Harvey to summon the discipline to study and achieve acceptable grades. He therefore dropped out of college after the first semester. He worked for a short while selling silk hosiery door-to-door. He then went to work at Gillette's Dairy in Missouri Valley, Iowa, as a deliveryman for ten dollars a week. He also worked as a volunteer fireman, which covered the cost of his room. It was during this time that he met Wilma Jones, who was boarding with our uncle John (my mother's brother) and aunt Marie while she taught at Bennett School, which my brothers and sisters and I all attended. My father, who was the school director, hired Wilma. After being introduced to Harvey, she sought to be with him as much as possible. She quit teaching the year I started attending Bennett School and attended nurses training for six months. Following that, she became a nanny, caring for three children.

Harvey and Wilma were married while he worked at Gillette's Dairy, pinching pennies to get by. From there, he went to work for Robert's Dairy in Omaha. Wilma became pregnant a few months later. Near her delivery date, my mother and I went to visit Harvey and Wilma. Their Christmas tree was lit with many beautiful lights, which enhanced this joyous time of anticipation of their new arrival.

My mother and I left after a couple of days with great joy and excitement over the baby's impending arrival. Wilma was looking forward to delivering her firstborn after New Year's, and she hoped the baby would be lavished with gifts. But, tragically, I was awakened by my father during the night after New Year's and told the awful news of Wilma's and Harvey's baby boy, who was born under very difficult circumstances. The baby was unable to be delivered, and panic-stricken, the doctor fetched Harvey from the waiting room to help him pull the baby through the birth canal, since both Wilma and the baby would not survive if the baby was not delivered quickly. They pulled on the clamps attached to the baby's head. Wilma was nearly pulled from the table, and the baby's head finally emerged, but his neck was broken, and the beautiful baby emerged deceased.

Harvey and Wilma were devastated, but the baby's clothes were packed away and the burial decisions were made. Harvey's older sister Eva had coped with similar tragedies twice before she gave birth to her daughter Mary Ann. Thus, with great compassion, she took over to advise and assist Harvey and Wilma in dealing with this monumental task.

Time helped soothe the pain of this terrible loss. Harvey continued working for Robert's Dairy. His younger brother Chris came soon after to live with them to help my parents during the Great Depression. This left Ken, Henry, and me to be supported at home. Chris got along well with Wilma and Harvey. He had two paper routes, which paid for his expenses. He formed a bond with Wilma and Harvey and their children for the rest of his life.

On November 4, 1936, Wilma gave birth to Barbara without any problems. Harvey was at the height of his glory. He dearly loved Barbara, and the feeling was mutual. On July 10, 1938, Wilma had a very difficult time delivering her son Stan. He suffered a brain injury during birth. A specialist was called in to give every possible assistance to Stan. After finishing high school, Stan pursued a successful career working for Caterpillar, Inc., in Chicago. Eventually, Harvey became a sales manager for Robert's Dairy.

After Henry and Stella attended Morningside College and worked at Gillette's Dairy in Missouri Valley Iowa for a year, Harvey helped Henry move to Omaha, where he worked for Robert's Dairy. Harvey was a stabilizing influence for Henry. When Harvey was about seventeen or eighteen years old, before he met Wilma, he met a nurse named Luella while he was in the hospital recovering from an eye injury caused by a cat clawing him. He fell deeply in love and carried this romance in his heart for many years.

One memory I have of Harvey that stands out in my mind is the time my mother was chopping wood and a chip struck her above one of her eyes. The resulting large wound was bleeding profusely while she held her hand over her eye. She found her way into the house, ordering Esther to stop screaming and to help her. When the bleeding was under control, she called the high school to get word to Harvey to bring home gauze, tape, and a disinfectant. When Harvey arrived home and assessed the gaping wound, he refused to help, saying he was unable to do the job. But Mom firmly said that he had no choice. The amazing outcome was that Harvey taped the wound so well that the scar was only a very fine line that eventually disappeared completely.

Harvey was very endearing. I cannot recall Harvey ever acting unkindly toward me. He loved reading to my mom while she worked. However, he got into serious trouble with Henry one evening after Henry finished his chores while Harvey was reading to Mom. Henry was on the verge of beating him up for not doing his own chores.

I also remember the time I was invited to a birthday party at our neighbors', the Fuhrs. Birthday parties were a rarity and something to savor, but as I prepared to go, Harvey arrived unexpectedly. He was no longer living at home, and his visits were a wonderful treat. I left for the party, but when I arrived, I began to feel sad and then felt sick. I soon told Lottie Fuhr, the mother, that I was sick. She had me lie on her couch, where I overheard her say how hard it would be for my dad if I were to die. Not seeing any improvement in my condition, she gave my parents four short rings on the party line and then told my mother I was sick. Harvey arrived in a flash to drive me home. I was so proud of my big brother, and by the time I was home, I felt much better. My mother with her wisdom said she thought I just wanted to be with Harvey.

There was one incident that I recall when Harvey did not receive my father's usual favor. Harvey told me he had a bike and that he put a lock on it. A couple of my brothers cut the bicycle spokes to remove the lock. When Harvey expressed his sadness to Dad about what had happened, Dad said, "That is what you get for being selfish."

Many years later when my husband, Bill, and I moved to Seattle in 1970, Harvey and Wilma moved to Santa Cruz, California. We visited them with our sons Bill and Steve. Harvey loved both of them and promised to take them to a nudist beach, a promise that he fulfilled. We returned to Santa Cruz several times. Harvey and Wilma and Barbara's family came to my daughter Nancy's wedding in Seattle. Sadly, Harvey was developing advanced symptoms of Alzheimer's disease in his late sixties. His last trip to see us in Seattle was a dangerous drive. I believe he had Alzheimer's for approximately ten years, but during his last year, he deteriorated rapidly. Wilma and Barbara did their best to keep him home. He was in a nursing home for about eight months. Harvey was unable to swallow toward the end of his life and weighed only 145 pounds in his six-foot-three-inch frame. Harvey died at the age of seventy-two. I was glad to be able to fly down for his memorial service. He was a wonderfully special brother. He expressed his affections so very well and was attached to my mother as much as I was, and he shared with me how much he worried about Mom. Wilma told me she had never been really happy until she married Harvey.

Harold Kermit

My brother Harold was the first child born after my parents returned to America from Denmark. He was an easy child to raise until he went to high school. He was only five and a half feet tall when he started high school, and he was initiated by the upperclassmen with the use of heavy paddles. He found no reward in scholastic achievement, and the friends he associated with were poor role models. He made flippant remarks to some of his teachers and enjoyed creating whatever extra commotion drew laughs or attention from his fellow students. In his senior year, my father received phone calls from the superintendent warning him that Harold was flunking his courses. My father dealt with this issue by allowing the school to use any punishment they thought might be effective. As a result, Harold was punished with a large paddle. Fortunately, he graduated in 1932.

Harold believed that his father never acknowledged him for his work. My brother Harvey was a hard act to follow. My father trusted Harvey implicitly and often held back praise that Harold deserved for doing more than his share of work around the house. Harvey was never one to argue with his father and was able to appease his father's demands using diplomacy—even though he did not always carry out Dad's orders.

When Harold finally graduated from high school, he had grown to six feet three inches and was a handsome man. He had no goals or job prospects, and the Great Depression made jobs scarce or nonexistent. Many young men became vagrants, traveling on freight trains from city to city. Men would come begging for food. I remember my sister Eva serving food to vagrants on her sunporch. For a short time, Harold undertook the job of digging water wells. It was dangerous work, and my mother turned away any phone calls requesting this work. Harold was a hard worker, but he spent his money "living it up." He treated his brothers Harvey and Holger to nights out dancing. It was understood that if any fighting began after the men had consumed a few drinks, Harvey and Harold were to step in to assure that Holger's left eye was not injured, because of the blindness in his right eye. Holger and Harold also enjoyed hunting together.

Harold was two years younger than Harvey. My parents had taken "the big plunge" by buying a farm five miles from Missouri Valley, Iowa. Harold was the first child born on that farm, where the next five children were also born. Harold loved the land, and very early on showed his love of hunting. My parents gave Harold an old rusty shotgun for Christmas when he was only four years old. The gun was previously owned by Uncle John, my mother's brother. Harold had barely unwrapped the gun when he went off on a mission climbing the fence and dragging the gun behind him. This love of guns and hunting never left him. As he grew up, he was never happier than when he had his gun ready for his next adventure. From time to time, Holger accompanied Harold on his hunting trips. One of their adventures nearly ended in tragedy. They were supposed to return at an agreed-upon time set by my dad. They were sidetracked, possibly because a neighbor invited them into their house and offered them a few animals that were frozen. The animal skins would be valuable to their collection and could be sold at a future date. When they arrived home, my dad met them, shouting his anger because of their tardiness. He lunged at Holger, grabbed his shotgun, and threw it to the ground. The gun accidentally fired, scattering buckshot all around. Holger yelled as he fell to the ground. My father panicked, thinking he had killed his son. When Holger realized he was still alive, he looked around gratefully and rose to his feet. For a while, this incident left my father horrified, shaken, and very sobered by what he had done.

On another hunting trip, Harold was returning late in the evening, walking through unfamiliar territory, when his feet gave out from under him. He felt himself falling into what was an abandoned well. He was not seriously hurt, but he knew no one would ever find him. As Harold thought about his desperate circumstances, he wondered whether he could muster the strength and savvy to save himself by climbing out. As a result of his experiences building wells during the Great Depression, he knew something about how wells were constructed. Because of this knowledge, he was able to climb out by pressing his feet on opposite sides of the well, slowly bracing himself as he ascended to the surface. He eventually worked himself to the top, where Skeesix, the family dog, happily greeted him.

Harold also told us of another experience when he was confronted by a panther in the timbers at the top of the lane leading to our house. In desperation, he snapped his jacket at the panther and frantically ran toward our house, while Skeesix kept the animal at bay by barking at it. When Harold reached our fence, he was exhausted and fell over the top of the fence. It was later reported that a panther had been seen in the area of our farm. My mother said that one night, she heard what sounded like a baby crying and believed it was the panther. Also, I saw large animal tracks in the snow in the lane leaving our farm.

One winter, we were totally snowed in, and food supplies were running low. Harold offered to walk three miles across our fields to the small town of Loveland to get emergency supplies. The snow was waist-deep in some areas, and I think that if it hadn't been Harold who undertook this mission, my mother would have doubted the wisdom of the task. He not only completed the trip but proudly acknowledged carrying a full fifty-pound sack of flour rather than giving up, like our neighbor Conrad Fuhr, who carried only a small portion of flour home. Harold returned exhausted and demanded some of the whiskey that Mom kept for medicinal purposes. He begged and ranted for the whiskey, but she never gave it to him.

Another incident involving Harold occurred when the stovepipes connecting our cooking stove to the chimney became clogged with soot. My mom and I suspected there was a problem when we heard crackling sounds in the kitchen stovepipe. Shortly after we heard the sounds, fire began shooting out of our chimney, sending sparks onto the dry roof. Mother told me to run out and get Harold and Henry, who were in the field. I ran outside shouting, "Fire, fire!" When they heard me, Harold jumped from the machine he was on and sprinted home, while Henry just leisurely walked back to the house. Harold climbed onto the roof with a sack of sand and managed to put out the fire as we and the neighbors looked on. Glowing cinders were flying all around Harold. Just as he was finishing, his feet slid out from under him and he slid off the roof, hitting the ground. Fortunately, one of our neighbors broke his fall to the cement below. Henry later said that my cries of "fire" were no more frightening to him than if I had said that Dad just came home.

Money was always in short supply during the Depression, and Harold wanted Mom to loan him cash for a trip into town. She responded firmly that she had no money, but feeling important because I had something that was in such great demand, I told Harold, "Well, I have forty-eight cents on the shelf under the clock!" Harold responded, saying, "Are you crazy? I already took that money!"

Harold enjoyed our horses a great deal. He and Henry usually broke the horses for riding. Harold attempted to stand with one foot on each of the horses as he held the bridles in both hands. On one occasion when one of our colts was on the verge of dying due to an intestinal blockage with chaff, it was decided that Ken's and my hands and arms were small enough that if we reached in, we could clear the blockage. Ken flatly refused. I was then asked to do the dirty work, and I agreed. Ken couldn't watch me do it. I was firmly taken to the barn while Harold, Henry, Mom, and Dad looked on in anticipation. When I realized what exactly I had to do, I exclaimed, "I can't do it!" My poor mother panicked and tried to work her fingers into the colt to decrease the tension that was building. But her hands were nearly as big as my dad's. Everyone was dismayed by what they were seeing, but Henry was outraged. Henry took me back to the house with a very firm hand, and he told Ken that he had no choice but to do the job. Ken cooperated knowing there was no way he could get away with saying no to Henry. After Ken's attempt, he went back to the house with his arm covered with the colt's feces. I had to turn my head to avoid getting sick. After Ken washed himself, I looked at him and saw a small amount of waste still on him; I pointed to it and started to gag. Sadly, after all of the attempts to relieve the blockage, the little colt died.

The Depression exacerbated evening arguments between Dad and Harold. Harold had a few wild friends, and one evening he came home drunk. Since my dad's father was an alcoholic, seeing Harold drunk was harder for him to take. Dad thought Harold was going nowhere in life. Harold had a poor opinion of himself. During one of Dad's many arguments with Harold, he became so deeply hurt by Dad's assessment of him that he decided to leave and said he was never coming back. My mother cried and convinced my dad to try to reach him at his friend Dan Ryan's home. My dad subsequently apologized, and Harold returned home.

Harold often played his harmonica in the evening, which would turn my melancholia into deep sadness. My solution was to hide his harmonica, but he always knew I hid it and forced me to find it. Harold had a beautiful singing voice as well as the ability to yodel. When Harold left home four years after graduating from high school, the Great Depression was easing. He took a job in Omaha working for The Prudential Insurance Company, where he met his future wife, Norma Engel. They married after dating a few months. They had a daughter, Nancy, born in August 1940 and a son, Larry, born in August 1941. However, Harold's resolve to get on his feet wasn't working, and he was still drinking, so he moved with his family to Los Angeles, vowing to save enough money to buy a farm. He worked two jobs at the Wonder Bakery. By 1944, he had saved enough money to move back to Iowa and buy his first farm. A few years later, he moved to a larger farm and was very successful. Around this time, Harold and Norma had their third child, Ben. Despite these successes, Harold's restlessness continued, and he was unable to give up his excessive drinking.

Norma was a patient wife, but her health began to fail. She developed emphysema and died several years before Harold did. Harold continued working his farm, living alone. One day, he returned from a trip to town, forgetting to set the brakes on his truck, which started to roll. He tried to jump into the cab, but he fell. The truck ran over him. He lay on the ground for hours. His grandson was alerted by a friend who was concerned when Harold did not answer his phone. Harold's first words were, "Get a stick so I can kill this damn dog!"

The dog had been licking him the whole time he was lying on the ground. Harold was then hospitalized and seemed to be recovering, but he died suddenly on December 26, 1998, probably due to a blood clot. During his hospitalization, an x-ray showed what was apparently a spot on his lung, which was believed to be cancer. He had been a heavy smoker and quit only late in life.

Esther Marie

My earliest memory of Esther was the great kindness she showed to me and others around her. She was truly my advocate, and I loved her more than I did any other person, except for my mother. I remember when she had to leave home to room and board at my sister Eva's house while Esther attended high school. Esther was also an advocate for Ardelle and LaVonne who were Eva's stepdaughters. After two years, Esther went to work for Eva's friend Gertrude Brown, helping with the care of Gertrude's two sons. This was a reprieve for Esther compared with life under the same roof with Howard.

Every time Esther returned home for a day or two, she would surprise Ken and me with a gift. I have vivid memories of the time when my mother left for the hospital to have gallstone surgery. I was a young child in despair, thinking she was going to be butchered just like the animals on our farm that I had watched being cut open as they were butchered. I was upset and inconsolable, and Ken found me crying. He promptly reported my fears to Esther. In her kindly manner and with great empathy, she explained that my mother was going to be given the care that would heal her so she could come back home. It is not possible to fully explain how secure and assured I then felt— sure that all would be well. She provided Ken and me with much-needed security. Esther was also willing to come home whenever there was an emergency. When my mother became very ill, possibly with pneumonia, Ken and I took turns staying home from school to pick up wood chips to keep the fire going in our large cookstove. I was relieved when Esther came home from nurses' training to assume responsibility for everything.

I recall how sad I was when Esther graduated from high school and left home to start nurses' training in Council Bluffs, Iowa, about thirty miles away. I had the feeling this meant I would not see her for a long time, and possibly only a few times before she graduated. As a result, I felt and looked ill. Upon Esther's first visit home, I suddenly perked up, and my mother realized I had been grieving over Esther's absence. I was surprised that my mother had not been aware of the reason for my sadness. When Ken was born, Mom delegated the responsibility of caring for him to Esther, who bonded to Ken like a mother. When Esther went to visit Eva and her first husband, she felt desperate and needed to visit home to see that he was all right.

When I was about four years old, Esther and my brother Harold had an angry confrontation while she was mopping the kitchen floor. Harold was sitting nearby, recuperating from chicken pox. I had pinkeye and walked over to Harold, who shoved me away, in frustration because I had already given him chicken pox. Esther was outraged at his lack of kindness. As a result, she grabbed the bucket of soapy water and threw it all over Harold. Fortunately, Dad came home that very minute and saved Esther from what would have been a disastrous reaction from Harold.

I had seen the two beautiful dolls that LaVonne and Ardelle were given, and I expressed how much I wanted a doll just like theirs. On her next trip home, Esther arrived with a large box that she claimed was a new dress for herself; she told me that if I washed my hands, I could see it. I repeated my desire for a doll like LaVonne's and Ardelle's. She then brought me the box to show me her dress. When I opened it and saw the doll I wanted so badly, I was ecstatic, and my love for my wonderful sister had no bounds.

On another occasion, Esther told me that when I was a small child my neck beneath my hair perspired, and that reminded her of the down of a little chick.

When Esther grew to the age when she could start dating, Holger told her that she should not marry the first man who came along, like her two older sisters Eva and Ragnhild had. She followed his advice and dated many young men. She loved dancing as much as my father did, and this caused Dad a lot of concern, wondering where those dances were held. But Dad's concerns never slowed her down. She mastered the Charleston and every other dance that was popular at the time.

Esther was a beauty. Holger's wife, Viola, who was in nurses' training with her, said Esther could have had any man she wanted. Because Esther was also very feisty, my father advised her that, before she started nurses' training, she would have to learn to take orders. One day while we were sitting on our porch, my father became wild-eyed when Esther declared she would never take orders from anyone. My father shouted back, "You will take orders, or I will whack you so hard, you'll roll over three times!"

Esther shared many of her experiences in nurses' training at the hospital, which I found to be extremely interesting. I loved hearing about anything associated with health and medicine. During her last year in nursing school, Esther met her future husband, John Linder. John noticed her when she was on a walk and stopped her to ask directions to a cemetery. While she tried to explain, he suggested that she get into his car and show him how to get there. Of course, it was a ploy, but it served him well, because they started dating.

John's parents were no longer living but he had inherited a small fortune. In addition, John owned a beer distribution business, a number of houses, and flew his own plane. Ken and I were fascinated when, one day, he flew over our house and dropped a note in a tin can to the ground. John confessed to Esther that he was married with a young son but that he was planning a divorce. Months later, they were married and moved into John's family home in Council Bluffs, Iowa. Their first child, Joan, was born that fall and their second child, John, was born two years later. They moved to Missouri Valley after most of John's fortune was gone. John gave flying lessons and ran a gas station. Their third child, Jerry, was born there. Esther enjoyed being near our mother and enrolled in a nursing refresher course. John was a womanizer and was advised by people in Missouri Valley to leave the city. They moved to Kansas City, Missouri where Joan, John and Jerry finished elementary school and graduated with college degrees.

John eventually developed cancer, and Esther dedicated her life to helping him recuperate. He remained critically ill for many months. Following John's death, Esther was mentally and physically exhausted and felt lost. As a result, she stopped eating properly and was not well. Her neighbors contacted Esther's daughter, Joan, who was living in Chicago, and asked her to visit Esther and convince her to live with Joan. Esther agreed, but the time she spent living with Joan was stressful for both of them. Esther always gave a great deal of herself serving the needs of others but she was now spent and exhausted and lost all interest in cultivating friendships as she had in the past.

Esther's son John and his wife, Bonnie, lived in the island nation of Bahrain on the Persian Gulf. Despite the distance, they visited Esther every year. Esther occasionally visited her son Jerry and his family in St. Louis, Missouri, but she always felt insecure while she was away from home. On July 24, 1992, Esther died from a heart attack while sitting in her chair, watching TV. She was found by Joan's son Eric when he arrived home from an errand.

Henry Ellis

Henry was born on November 25, 1917. He was twelve pounds at birth, the largest of all the Andersens' ten children. He and Esther became close friends as small children. However, Esther grew closer to Harold in their teens, probably a result of their shared interests. Henry seldom appeared happy or to be having fun. He recounted that sledding had no purpose, because he had to pull the sled back up the hill over and over again. Henry had a close relationship with our mother. Once he picked wildflowers for her but was so dismayed when he discovered they had been thrown out that he threw a brick through a window to demonstrate his displeasure.

My mother tried to make up for my dad's strong discipline. Often, when Dad was gone, Henry and his brothers would take time off from their chores to enjoy her company. If Dad returned unexpectedly, they jumped out the kitchen window and headed back into the fields to resume their work.

Henry's greatest pleasure was his love of horses, especially the newborn colts. He and Harold broke the colts for riding. When the colts appeared sick, Henry became morose and wanted to have a veterinarian come out to examine them. I remember a large disagreement on this subject, ending with Henry punching the door with his fists as he left the house. But even in his frustration, he seemed to show a strong admiration for his dad. He once recalled my father explaining fencing techniques he used with swords in the Danish cavalry. Henry and his brothers practiced fencing with sticks until they developed enough confidence to show their skills to my dad. He also recalled a tender moment when my dad shared his remorse for describing his mother, who had tuberculosis, as a hunchback.

Once, my father became very angry after Henry stated that he felt belittled by him. Without further thought, my father spat on Henry. I always felt loved by Henry and believed his frantic outbursts were due to uncontrollable frustrations, and, therefore, I felt forgiveness toward him. I remember when Henry believed I was being untruthful with him, and he decided that I needed to recant what I had said. So he grabbed me and held my head over the open cookstove fire. For some reason, I remained confident during the ordeal and never flinched while dangling over the fire. My mother cried out, "Be careful, Henry! She is one who will not back down if she believes she is right." Harold added, "Henry, if her hair caught fire, you'd never forgive yourself!"

Whenever Henry was involved in an argument, he would typically shout out orders to everyone, and usually my brothers Ken and Chris were the victims. For example, during an argument about a neck yoke (a device used on a horse-drawn wagon), Ken sensed Henry's growing anger and became frantic. He grabbed the neck yoke and ran to a ditch to dispose of it. While doing their chores one evening, an argument ensued between Henry and Chris. Henry asked my mother to hold the lantern so he could kill Chris. Chris always remained quiet during these episodes. During another incident, our cat killed one of Henry's pigeons, which he enjoyed and kept in special houses he constructed. Henry became enraged and said he would shoot the cat. Ken pleaded with Henry, saying it was in the nature of cats to attack birds, but his pleas had no effect. Ken carried the cat over a mile away, hoping it would not return. But the cat found its way back to our house, and Henry proceeded to shoot it.

Henry never dated while he was in high school. He walked the five miles to school in every kind of weather. Since Henry waited a year before starting high school and Chris skipped a grade, they spent two years in high school in the same grade. I remember overhearing them in bed at the end of the day sharing some of their experiences. The two of them were very different. Even though Henry appeared overly constrained and very frustrated at home, he seemed to need the security. It was during the Great Depression that my brother Harvey and his wife, Wilma, offered Henry the opportunity to live with them in Omaha during the last two years of high school, to help my parents. Henry refused the offer, so Chris went instead. Henry took the Great Depression very seriously, concerned about the toll it took on my mother, as well as on my brother Ken and me. Karen, Henry's daughter, recollected how my mother appealed to Henry out of desperation, having hardly anything to fix for dinner. She chose to first protect my father, with Henry's support. My parents had so little money that my teeth became badly decayed and were not repaired. I remember when Henry expressed great concern for my well-being, fearing I would develop a serious health problem, which he described as a "leakage of the heart."

Henry resented the fact that Holger was in college during this time, believing that the little money my parents gave Holger should have been used at home to help with the family's needs. My mother felt strongly that Holger would not find another niche in life if he were denied the opportunity to pursue his love of medicine. After Henry graduated from high school, he chose to work on our farm for a year in order to save money for college. At the end of the year, he started attending Morningside College in Sioux City, Iowa. I believe this was the first time that Henry began to enjoy life. He met Stella Isenberger, with whom he fell deeply in love. During his first visit home, I noticed he no longer enjoyed cowboy music but now listened to the popular songs on the *Hit Parade*, a radio music program. I thought to myself that this was what I had expected to happen. He became more polished, and we no longer shared the enjoyment of country music. Still, he was very sweet to me, and I felt important to him. As the year progressed, he and Stella became more serious, and eventually he brought her home one weekend so that all of us could meet her. When Henry requested privacy so that he and Stella could be alone in the dining room, Ken and I peeked through the keyhole to see what they were up to. Chris, who came home that same weekend, enjoyed our reports about their amorous gestures.

When Henry finished his first year at college, he and Stella made plans for marriage. Henry received letters from Stella, which I managed to get into. When he noticed the letters were mixed up, my snooping was followed by threats of dire consequences. Undeterred, I made sure I put them back in the same order the next time.

Henry and Stella were married in the fall of 1939. Henry earned ten dollars a week at Gillette's Dairy, just as Harvey had after his marriage. Kenneth stayed with them during his first year in high school. They were very kind to Ken. At the end of that year, Henry went to work at Robert's Dairy in Omaha delivering milk, where Harvey was now an executive. Stella enjoyed Omaha, but Henry had trouble with the early hours, and he made up for it by sleeping during the day after work. He suffered from headaches and sinus problems, as well as from depression. Their daughter Karen was born in Omaha on May 11, 1940.

My parents were retiring to Missouri Valley, and my father, worried about Henry's health, proposed that Henry move to our farm. Henry's son Lynn was born on our farm. Henry was still having trouble getting up early. Stella often started the day ahead of him by getting the cows ready for milking. Henry occasionally went hunting during this time. Raccoon hunting was popular, and I think Harold and Henry enjoyed doing this together along with friends. My mother decided to sell the farm a few years after my father's death. She needed the money for her support. Henry and Stella then moved to Logan, Iowa, and began renting a farm from Howard Nelson, my sister Eva's second husband. Their son Grant was born on August 1, 1950. Henry was not given to good financial planning. He worked hard at farming but never seemed to be able to get ahead. He was not a good manager. Stella was a good helper, as was Karen, their daughter. In the end, Stella and Karen worked harder than they should have worked.

Henry was inclined to be critical of his children. He often told Karen and Lynn that they would never amount to anything. When Karen shared her desire go on to college, he suggested that she was not smart enough. I somehow believe that he had such low self-esteem that he believed his offspring were unable to achieve anything, simply because they were his children. Henry was not interested in a social life with Stella, but he enjoyed contact with the neighbors. He enjoyed helping them with their farming needs. Stella traveled alone to England while Karen and her husband were stationed there. Henry would never have considered traveling himself.

Henry was very controlling of Grant and trusted that he was college material, so Grant received the support he needed and was able to graduate from college. Henry developed asthma and high blood pressure, and the decision was made to move to the town of Logan. They had bought a house there earlier. After retirement, Henry felt useless. Because of his poor health, he was unable to maintain their small yard. He was embarrassed when people saw that Stella was taking care of most of the yard work. He did enjoy taking walks and often stopped to talk with neighbors.

Ken said that during one of his last visits with Henry, Henry expressed remorse as he looked back over his life. He felt that he was unsuccessful in accomplishing what he would have liked to achieve. Ken explained to him that most people have this feeling late in life, and he told Henry to take heart in the things he did accomplish. One day, at sixty-eight years old, Henry experienced severe chest pain. Stella called an ambulance. When the ambulance arrived, Henry refused to be carried out of the house. He instead walked to the ambulance, but he died before he reached the hospital. I realize that during all his years, he greatly wanted reassurance from my mother, and Stella did much to take my mother's place. Henry was not an easy husband to live with, but he relied heavily on Stella being there for him.

Chris Jr. Elmer

As I think about my brother Chris, my memories are of someone who was there a lot but was usually on the periphery. Henry and Harold were around at the same time and seemed to demand and get much more attention. Chris was the baby for five years before Ken was born. Therefore, my mother had a greater opportunity to spend time with Chris than she did with her other children. Chris was very close to my mother. I cannot remember him ever sassing her. It was obvious that he carried concern as well as love for her. It was very difficult for Chris to disappoint his mother. When Chris was a baby, my mother talked about his sweet velvet bottom as she changed his diaper. Overhearing this, Esther and Henry attempted to makes things more equal by taking my father's farm file and roughening Chris's bottom with it.

Chris enjoyed helping my mom around the house, but he expressed anger and frustration with my dad. He never confronted my father, but instead made fun of him and his Danish accent behind his back. I have no recollection of Chris arguing with any of his siblings or our parents. He was silent much of the time, but was obviously a very angry person. He impressed me as someone who felt that strictly controlling his anger was the only way to behave without being fearful. However, his frustration and anger were evident in his relationship with Ken and me.

Ken and I had attention from my mom that Chris would have liked for himself. One evening when I was about four years old, I burst into laughter during dinner. Chris grabbed the pepper shaker and shoved it under my nose, which quickly turned my laughter into tears. After the evening meals, I would occasionally lie on a bench my mother and I shared, with my head on her lap while she stroked my head. I believe

Chris looked at me and silently wished it was he and not I who was lying there.

When Ken started school, Chris was ten years old and behaved as though he "knew the ropes." Chris obviously felt in control. On the way to school, a large red bull would try to break through a fence. Ken was absolutely terrified by the bull, while Chris ran away from his brother. Ken's fear of the bull became such a problem that my mother allowed him to skip school one day.

Chris enjoyed playing tricks on others and seemed to have a superior attitude. On a cold winter day on the way to school, he suggested that our neighbor Robert Fuhr pick up a "rock" that Chris spied at the side of the road for his rock collection. Robert put the rock in his pocket for safekeeping. As the day wore on, a stench developed near Robert, and much to his surprise and frustration, the prized rock, which was actually a piece of frozen manure, melted. Chris was very bright and skipped a grade, starting high school at the age of twelve. He and Henry walked five miles each way throughout the school year in winter temperatures that often were below zero, as well as in the spring heat. I think Chris was not one to complain; whatever he felt was not expressed outwardly.

One of Chris's favorite ways of frustrating me was by making faces. If I didn't respond, he would move closer to me, almost rubbing noses. Once when he tried to frustrate me several times during the day, I burst into tears. My father quickly responded, and Chris just as quickly disappeared. Chris was very adept at bargain shopping, and Harold enlisted him one Christmas to do all of his gift shopping. When I opened Harold's gift to me, I was thrilled. Harold, who was sitting near me, asked who had given me the gift. He had not bothered to check the gifts with Chris, who probably wrapped the gifts as well.

Chris was much more fun to be around than Ken and Henry were. My father bought me roller skates after I had learned how to skate in school using a friend's pair of skates. Chris was impressed with my ability to skate, and he may have tried my skates.

As a child, I feared sleeping alone in my bedroom. One night, Henry decided that Chris was too warm for him to sleep with, so he asked Ken to trade places with Chris. I objected because I also thought Chris was too warm. Therefore, I immediately called my mother, saying I wanted to sleep with Ken. I left the room because of my complaint and returned when Henry told me to come back. Chris was sleeping with him. I happily returned when I heard laughter from Henry's bed. Ken was unable to contain himself in having tricked me. Chris was quiet through all of this, going from one bed to the other and finally sleeping with Henry. Soon after all of this happened, my mother gave me no choice but to move into my own bedroom and to sleep alone.

My step-niece Ardelle was easily frightened. During a visit to my sister Eva, Chris was pretending to admire Ardelle's skillful piano playing. As he stood there and watched, he slowly lowered a box he was holding and emptied the contents onto the piano keys. A huge bull snake slid across the keys. Ardelle screamed and disappeared.

On another occasion I recall that Chris had a serious infection near his nose. It was so bad that his face became distorted from the severe swelling. He was fortunate to have survived, because there were no antibiotics in those days. When Chris was fourteen, he left home to live with Harvey and Wilma in Omaha. As I've mentioned previously, in order to help my parents during the Depression, Harvey had asked Henry to stay with them. Since Henry chose not to go, Chris decided he would go instead.

Chris worked very hard, having two paper routes—one in the morning and one in the afternoon—and earning thirty-five dollars each month, which was an excellent salary at that time. He took care of all his personal expenses and adjusted well to living there. He and Wilma got along well. She remembered when Chris confronted two young men who made unkind remarks about Wilma's fat pregnant body.

I remember Chris hitchhiking home one weekend to see us. He brought Ken and me a ring-toss game. He was very happy to see us, showing a touch of sadness at being away from us. I was very sad when he left, thinking he would have to hitchhike back and that I would miss him.

Chris worked on a farm near us for a year, so that he could save money for college. He and Henry started college at Morningside, in Sioux City, Iowa. After being there for a year, Chris enrolled at the University of Iowa in Iowa City. He spent much of his available time working in Holger's office during the summer months while Chris prepared for medical school. When I was thirteen years old, I spent several weeks living with Holger and Viola while Chris was there. I was responsible for most of ten-month-old Jon's care for about two weeks while Holger and Viola were gone. Chris was assigned the care of Holger's office. He and I enjoyed that time, and we got along very well. I met his girlfriend, Donna Fredricks, when she was about sixteen years old. Chris and Donna eventually married.

After two years at the University of Iowa, Chris started medical school. During his first year, he was expelled. I recall being told about an incident in his anatomy class, where he threw a piece of a cadaver at another student just when the professor entered the room, hitting the professor instead. I don't think Chris was ever able to cope with having been dismissed from medical school. World War II had just begun, and Chris joined the US Air Force as a second lieutenant. Donna was in nurses' training, but she dropped out and eloped with Chris.

Chris was stationed at March Field in California when I visited him and Donna. I went instead of my mother, who was invited but chose not to go. I was entering my senior year in high school and was ecstatic to have this opportunity. Looking back, I see the mistake my mother and I made in assuming it was all right to ask if I could come in her place. Because Chris was unable to disappoint his mother, he waited a long time to answer our query, but finally agreed it was all right. After a month, Donna was unhappy sharing their small apartment with me, and Chris felt under a lot of pressure. One evening, he told me I had to go home. I had just received my first paycheck from my job on the base doing typing for two lieutenants. Chris said I could use the money I had made for my ticket home. I cried and pleaded with Chris, but there was no changing his mind. The following day, I received a phone call at work from Chris, saying he had a letter from my father suggesting I move into another place close to them. Chris said if I could find another place in a week, I could stay. I found a temporary place for a week with several sisters from Minnesota who worked at the base. Shortly thereafter, I found a permanent place to stay. I remember going to an officers' dance after I had moved out. Chris also attended the affair, and he asked me to dance. He said he felt closer to me than he did to Donna, because, after all, he had known me for so much longer.

I had been dating Bart Lane and introduced him to Chris before Chris left on an assignment for a few months. Bart and I were soon spending all the time we could together. I was fascinated with Bart's honesty, integrity, and sincerity. I had never met anyone like him. Shortly after we met, he was matched with the crew he was going to be with as a B-24 copilot. He was assigned to active duty overseas after he completed his training. I dreaded the thought of his leaving. We made the decision to marry. We spent four weeks together before he left. The minister on the base suggested that I ask Donna to walk down the aisle with me. She was there at my request and treated Bart and me with respect.

I don't think I saw Chris again until I came home after my first year in college at the University of Washington. My mother spoke of my high grade point average, which Chris acknowledged. During the year I spent living with the Lanes while attending college, Chris wrote me a very unkind letter reprimanding me for discussing my sadness with my mother in letters I wrote to her during the time that Bart was missing in action. He also said I owed him money because he paid part of my rent to the person who shared the apartment with me. This was not true, and I was shaken by his dishonesty.

Chris left the service in 1946. He worked in sales for a while before he returned to the military during the Korean War in 1950. During this time in the service, he received his bachelor's degree. He attended the University of Nebraska in Lincoln. In 1956, he was able to get his master's degree while working in industrial management, still in the service. When Chris and Donna were at Chanute Field, my second husband, Bill Love, and I saw them often, since we were both at the University of Illinois. Bill was working toward his PhD in theoretical and applied mechanics. We enjoyed their visits. Chris was fascinated with my daughter Jean, who was two years old at the time. Among the many fun times we shared with them, I recall the time he told Jean her hands were "meat hooks." He bought Jean a tricycle as well as two fancy dresses. Chris offered to paint the interior of the barracks we lived in, which the university made available to veterans. He did a beautiful job, and the fresh coat of paint made the barracks more livable.

Both Chris and Donna loved children, and they adopted a newborn child. However, the parents changed their minds a couple of days after Chris and Donna took possession of the baby. It was a crushing blow to them. Their lives became very lonesome and conflicted, and they both began drinking heavily. Donna left Chris for another officer that she was seeing, and she followed this man and his children to Europe. Before Donna left Chris, she belittled him by saying he could go to Ted's farm and slop pigs. Chris was completely broken by this and was hospitalized after suffering a nervous breakdown.

Chris remarried a short time after retiring from the army as a lieutenant colonel, but the marriage failed. He then decided to move to Center Point, Iowa, to be close to Ken. There he met Ken's secretary, Norma, who was a very genuine and responsible woman. Chris sincerely loved her. She was previously married and had children and grandchildren. Chris finally had the family he had always wished for. They were planning to move to Texas to be near Norma's grandchildren, but Chris's health was failing. He was concerned and therefore asked Ken what his long-term prognosis was. He and Norma were married for only a few years. During this time, Chris taught for several years at Coe College. After Chris's death, Ken told me that Chris was fondly remembered by many of his students. Ken's grandson stopped by regularly at Chris's house on the way to school, and Chris would make breakfast for him. He and Norma were actively involved sponsoring a Vietnamese family. Ken housed the family in the basement of his medical building. Chris died on January 27, 1980, the day after his sixtieth birthday. I received a birthday card from him on February 3 (my birthday). I felt great sadness that we never became close. I believe Chris had poor self-worth and a fragile psyche that was easily crushed. As a result, he resorted to using lies to elevate people's opinion of him.

The evening Chris died, he and Norma were watching a TV program in bed. He was falling asleep and asked Norma to tell him how the program turned out. Shortly thereafter, Norma heard a suspicious sound in his breathing. She immediately called Ken, who came at once and determined that Chris had died. He said he looked at Chris and realized how all of their differences now seemed so unimportant.

Chris donated his body to the University of Iowa medical school. Before he died, he joked that he was going to get into medical school one way or another.

Donna's relationship with the officer she joined in Europe was unsuccessful. His children did not accept her. Donna's continued use of alcohol was her way of coping. Her brother went to England to bring Donna back to the United States. At that time, Chris had not yet married Norma, and Donna asked him if he wanted to try another go-around. Chris was not interested. Donna and a former priest became friends. He resembled Chris. On one of his visits to see Donna, her friend found Donna unconscious. She was in a coma. She was later diagnosed with a brain tumor and spent her last months in a nursing home.

As I write about my brother Chris's misfortunes, I am reminded of a quote that our favorite minister in Seattle, Harvey Buer, often recited to the congregation: "Life is short, and we do not have much time to be a blessing to others. So be quick to gladden the heart of those who travel the way with us. Be swift to love and make haste to be kind."

Kenneth Niels

Ken was the second to the last child born in our family of ten children. Ken and I were born at a time when both of our parents were being tested by their advancing age, as well as by the Great Depression. Both of these factors made each day filled with concern, but also determination. Eva had lost her husband when Ken was less than two years old; that loss was followed by the loss of her child, which made the times very difficult for our family. My older siblings pointed out our flaws to our parents, criticizing our capabilities. As a result, Ken and I both had doubts about our competence and self-worth. We became each other's advocates, but we also argued and fought a great deal. My father enjoyed taking me into town with him, leaving Ken to stay at home to help his brothers. After we were grown, Ken told me that in one summer, he counted thirty-two trips into town by me and my father. Ken was very serious and did not know how to play with friends. He was thrown together with five brothers and had to modify his behavior to win their approval.

Although Chris and Henry were closest in age to Ken, they both suffered from their own frustrations, and Ken had to bear their constant disapproval. Chris was displaced from a close relationship with his mother when Ken was born, leading to his resentment of Ken. When Ken started school, he and Chris had to walk by a pasture with an angry big red bull that charged the fence, pawing the ground. Ken became frantic with fear. Chris decided to run away, abandoning Ken.

Although Henry felt protective of Ken and me, his bad temper demanded a prompt response, which caused Ken near panic. One time, Henry and Chris decided to test Ken's strength by pitting him against a cousin in a mock prizefight. Ken dreaded what lay ahead, but he tried not to disappoint his brothers. They sat cheering for the one each wanted to win the fight. Ken was punched and bruised, ending up with a bloody nose. After the fight, Harold came by and sympathetically washed the blood off Ken's face.

I cannot remember a single incident when Ken instigated a fight or argument with anyone at school. I was more likely to fall into that role if I were challenged. I worried one time when I saw Ken being goaded into a confrontation. It was completely out of character for Ken to be an aggressor. I was uncertain how the confrontation would end if Ken were pushed too far. Ken was called "the professor" in grade school because of his studious demeanor and because he would seize an opportunity to espouse what he knew. His intellectual curiosity led him to buy the complete works of Shakespeare when he was around thirteen years old.

Ken was eager to save his money even when he was very young. He and I gathered black walnuts, shelled them, and sold the walnuts to whomever in the family would be swayed by his enthusiasm. He and I also set up a "store" to sell goodies that we had bought (unfortunately, I soon decided that it was more fun to eat the goodies than to sell them). Our dad was our first customer, choosing a cone with a candy topping made to look like ice cream. As I saw him walk away with this tempting treat, I suggested we eat everything instead of selling it. That made Ken very aggravated with me.

Another of my memories involves a time when one of our setting hens came out of the weeds with two baby chicks she had hatched. Ken and I adopted them. They were wonderful pets that followed us everywhere. Ken's chick disappeared, and he was crushed. I felt his sadness and offered to give him my chick. He refused the offer. In any event, my chick must have joined the pack, because it disappeared as well.

From the time we were young children, Ken said he wanted to be a doctor. He said that his interest in medicine was sparked after his older brother Holger became a physician. Ken wanted to follow in Holger's footsteps.

I don't remember Ken having a single close friend, but it didn't appear to bother him. He always seemed more focused on the future and what he had to do to achieve his goals.

We used to cut across our field on our way to the small town of Loveland, where we attended Sunday school. It wasn't something we looked forward to, but it offered us a change in our daily routines and left us with fond memories.

Ken and I loved all types of sweets. We both remember going to functions where we stuffed ourselves with desserts. Even so, we awoke the next day wishing we were able to eat more. One of my most touching memories is when Ken brought home half a marshmallow for me from a school party. He had never tasted a marshmallow before, and he enjoyed it so much, he wanted me to share the taste.

Ken took his responsibilities very seriously. One summer, he found a bloated cow in the field and realized she was going to die if she wasn't relieved of the gas. He desperately drove the cow home before she lay down. My mother and I could hear him howling as he approached the house with the cow. Mom rushed to get one of her long kitchen knives, which they drove into the hip area of the cow. The gas spewed out into the air with bits of sweet clover that had caused it.

In another incident, Ken came home from the field, covered with dirt and with torn trousers. He had been using a large rake in the field when the horses suddenly became spooked. The horses ran wildly out of control, with Ken screaming and pulling on the reins for dear life. They were finally stopped by a fence. Ken was extremely shaken and completely exhausted as he described what had happened.

Ken started high school three years before I did. Holger gave him a bicycle for the five-mile trip to school, but bad weather and the distance often made the journey very difficult. Ken spent most of his first year of high school with Henry and Stella, who were newly married and living in Missouri Valley. I was enthused about Ken's new life in high school. On one occasion, he agreed to take me to an opera performed at the high school. As we entered and he took a seat, I slid in beside him. He jumped up and ran to another seat as I followed close behind. My pride pushed me to follow once again. The game of musical chairs continued until I gave up, knowing we had created a comical scene. He said he didn't want anyone to think that I was his girlfriend.

Later, when I was a high school freshman, he probably would not have minded my presence. He proudly shared with me that one of his friends had commented that I was the prettiest girl there. At midyear of my first year in high school, my parents moved to Missouri Valley. Ken and I lived in the house (sold to us by Howard Nelson) for a few weeks before our parents joined us. When spring came, Ken made plans to attend the University of Iowa the following fall. He decided to work for Holger that summer to save money for college. This would be the first time he worked for anyone other than my dad, whom he regularly helped with his masonry work.

I remember the Sunday when Ken left for college after he graduated from high school. He and Dad departed for Holger's home. As they left, I suddenly realized how lonesome it was going to be without Ken around, and I knew that we would never again be together at home. I felt as if I would never grow accustomed to being the only sibling at home with my parents. As I cried, my mother suggested that we should get ready for church, assuring me this would help me feel better. Nevertheless, it was not the same after Ken left. Although we had never been socially connected, there was a void in my life without him.

Viola drove Ken to the University of Iowa in the fall of 1942 and helped Ken enroll. His tuition was reduced from $65 to $35 because of our father's poor financial status. Ken had only $126 for his first year at college. He received $40 each month from my brother Chris who owed money to Holger. At the end of the school year, he was drafted into the armed services in field artillery. Ken was devastated, because he had planned to go into the premed program. His basic training was to last seven to eight months, but he contracted scarlet fever after six months. As a result, he was forced to repeat basic training. He was hospitalized a second time, which required yet another repetition of basic training. He was scheduled to go overseas after his third basic training was completed. My mother asked Holger to intervene (Holger was an officer in the medical corps) by appealing to Ken's superiors to allow him to go back to college. At first, Holger was irritated at the request and believed Ken should accept his fate. When my mother expressed her frustration with Holger's response, he gave his full attention to the matter and appealed to a legal officer at Camp Crowder, where Holger was stationed. A letter was sent through the chain of command and ultimately to Ken's superiors. Holger suggested that Ken could serve his country better as a physician. Ken was then allowed to resume his education under the Army Specialized Training Program (ASTP). He was sent to the University of Pennsylvania to finish his premedical training and then to the Johns Hopkins University to attend medical school. When he graduated from Johns Hopkins, he began a rotating internship at the University of Iowa until 1950. He spent his general practice residency at St. Luke's Hospital in Cedar Rapids until 1951, when he moved to Center Point. His debt to the federal government for his medical education was forgiven.

During his medical practice, Ken treated six generations of one family. He practiced for almost fifty-one years until his retirement in 2001. He made it known to his medical practice staff that they were never to refuse to see people who were concerned about their health or who otherwise insisted on seeing a doctor. He saved a number of lives because of this policy. In one case, a woman had an ectopic pregnancy (where the embryo implants outside the uterus) and was unable to find a doctor who would see her. In desperation, she began telephoning doctors alphabetically. Ken agreed to see her and made the diagnosis, which required immediate surgery to save her life.

In 1998, Ken began volunteering at a community health service free clinic during the days off from his regular practice. He continued this volunteer work until 2006. He since has taken on the responsibility of signing patient prescription drug forms, requiring many extra hours of work each evening. Following his retirement, Ken and his wife Marilyn established the Dr. Kenneth N. Andersen Family Scholarship Trust. The trust provides three, $3,300 scholarships to high school graduates from the Center Point—Urbana school district. Ken wants to encourage young people from all walks of life to pursue higher education.

Ken's and Marilyn's children pursued their interests in college. Their daughter Holly became engrossed in a teaching career. Christa, also went into education but chose not to teach. Philip became a successful dentist. Ken Jr. completed medical school and joined a group practice as an internist in family medicine.

Marian Olivia

I felt a great deal of loneliness growing up. One of my early memories was the evening when my mother was sick at a time when I was very enthusiastic about attending a play at the Bennett Country School. She did not want me to go and appealed to me, saying she didn't feel well and needed me to stay home with her. I still remember suddenly feeling that nothing was as important as being there with my mother. My enthusiasm for the school program vanished.

Most of the time, things seemed very serious. I worried a great deal about my mother's health. She worked very hard and seemed very vulnerable. I knew that life was a struggle for her. As a result, if my parents had any disagreements, I stood up for my mother, regardless of the disagreement. My father used to say, "We won't ask Marian who she thinks is right, because we already know." It was hard for me to start school, because I did not want to leave my mother. I had to know exactly where she was, for her safety as well as for my own safety. Once, when I discovered that she was not going to be at home while I was away at school, I started crying. When the teacher asked me why I was crying, my reply was, "My mama went to town today," which didn't make a lot of sense to the teacher or anyone else.

As I grew older, I became more independent of my mother, but until I was seven or eight years old, I still felt panicked at the thought of losing her. Ken and I once wanted to do something special to surprise my mother. We didn't realize that the men's work shoes she wore to do her chores were worn out of necessity and not preference. We looked at the Sears catalog and tried to decide which of the men's shoes she would most like, but we didn't know her size. When we confessed why we wanted her shoe size, she was touched and smiled. She explained to us that wearing men's shoes was not her choice. She had only one pair of shoes to wear when she went out of the house, plus a pair of slippers to wear in the house. She got old work shoes from her sons, and she wore them while doing chores. I followed my mother outside a great deal when she did her chores. The farm seemed remote, and I loved the times when our families came together for visits. At times, I felt guilty when I encouraged people to stay longer, knowing it was harder for my mother.

Grade school was pleasant for me most of the time. I loved the spring when the fruit trees were blossoming and the birds were singing on my way to school. In spring, on the way home from school, Ken and I often stopped at a timber to pick blue violets and Dutchman's "britches," as well as mushrooms. School lasted from 9:00 a.m. to 4:00 p.m., including kindergarten, which also lasted a full day. We walked a mile and a half, which was okay when the weather was nice. But I remember that one day when I returned from school, Mother asked me if I had been able to keep warm that morning. She told me that the temperature was thirty degrees below zero. Spring thaws were dreadful for walking because every step meant tugging my boots from the soft mud. We weren't usually picked up if it rained, but I remember one time when my brother Harold brought a team of horses that were hooked up to a lumber wagon to save us from the rain. The wagon was open, but we covered ourselves with quilts that mother sent along with Harold.

As a kindergarten student, I learned phonics very well, and I also learned to read well. My father was very eager to have all of his children make him proud. At the end of kindergarten, our teacher, Miss Muller, decided to advance my friend Louise Ryan and me only to the first grade rather than to the second grade (it was typical in country schools to go directly to the second grade when you attended kindergarten for a full day). Her reasoning was obvious. Roger Nelson, who was the school director's son, had been sick that year and missed a great deal of school. The teacher obviously did not want to offend the school director, who would decide whether she would continue teaching the following year. This decision would not have mattered much, except my father could not handle the thought that one of his children was going to be held back. He was so disturbed by this that he made a special trip to the school to have a talk with the teacher. They spoke in a small foyer, where all of the students tried to hear the conversation. My father would not forgive me for the "disgrace" that he thought I brought to our family. He called me, "the valedictorian of the primer class," and my brother Chris followed suit.

I had many friends throughout grade school and looked forward to attending high school, thinking I would be with more-sophisticated city students. I spent half of my first year in high school staying at a distant cousin's house, Jeanette, working for room and board. Jeanette was the daughter of Aunt Carey, who had been like a second mother to my mother. Aunt Carey was bedridden, because one leg had been amputated due to diabetes and was under Jeanette's care. While I looked forward to my parents' plans to move to the city that spring, I had a lot of fun and enjoyed my friendships more than I did when I was living at home. Jeanette led the local chapter of Job's Daughters (an organization for young women), which gave me an inclusive feeling. Still, I felt self-conscious and unsure of myself. I believe this feeling developed when I started high school and began drawing a lot of attention, because I was attractive but did not have the confidence to deal with my good looks. I felt as if I didn't have what I needed to feel accepted by the popular group in high school. I wanted very much to be accepted but I was insecure, especially when I went to school assemblies by myself.

While I was in high school, I became somewhat interested in a student named Bob Birch, who showed a strong interest in me during my first year. He played first-string football, but I didn't think he was popular enough. He continued to be interested in me and quit high school in his junior year to join the US Army paratroopers. I was a junior in high school when he told me through a friend that he would like to write to me. We began writing each other, and I became more interested in him. Just before the junior prom, I did not know he would be home, and I asked a casual friend named Starchy Martin to escort me (Starchy was in Ken's grade). Bob was home on leave, and it saddened him when he heard about my decision, and he decided he would not call me. When I finally got in touch with him, he had only one night left before he would be leaving. We took in a movie, and he spent the evening with me afterward. My parents were very thoughtful and went to bed early. I felt sad that we did not get together sooner. Perhaps I loved him, but I was not *in* love with him. I doubted that he would be successful given his limited education.

I hardly dated in high school. I feared giving the impression that I was aggressive. One time when I attended a Job's Daughters dance, I wrote a letter to my date asking him to meet me there. I ended up dancing with a couple of high school graduates. My date asked me if I was with one of them. I don't think I made myself available enough for him to ask me to dance. My recollection is that we never danced. I didn't ask anyone whom I was interested in dating for fear they would think I was pursuing them.

I participated in one play in high school and sang in a mixed chorus. At the end of my sophomore year, I worked in Council Bluffs, which was thirty miles from my home, and then I worked at a wholesale drug company filling orders later that summer. The summer after my freshman year, I picked strawberries with my friend Donna Belle. I rather enjoyed that, though the summer was very boring overall. As I look back, high school was not fun for me. I have far better memories of my years in elementary school.

During my junior year in high school, my brother Chris and his wife, Donna, invited my mother to visit them in Riverside, California (as I've mentioned before). My mother asked me to write them to see if I could come instead. We waited a long time for their response, but they finally said yes. I left to visit them after school was out. I traveled with a friend, Mary Chisman, who was meeting her fiancé, a B-24 airplane bombardier-in-training. Mary had just graduated from high school. Later on, her husband completed his B-24 training and went to March Field before shipping out to England. He was a bombardier on a B-24 and was shot down on his third or fourth mission. He was taken prisoner but returned home after the war.

When I arrived at Riverside, I was fascinated with the beauty of Southern California. It was a whole new world to me. Donna and

Chris seemed pleased to see me. They had a small one-bedroom apartment with a couch in the living room, where I slept. I interviewed for a job at March Field a few days later and was fortunate to find a job within days. Two other women and I typed orders to Anchorage, Alaska, for supplies. A captain and a lieutenant were in charge of us. They were both very pleasant and made few if any demands on us. I loved going to the swimming pool and eating at the officers' club. It was more fun than I could ever remember having. I had worked long enough to receive my first paycheck when Chris told me one evening that I had to go home. Donna was unhappy having me there, and he had no recourse in making this decision. I wept and pleaded, but the decision stood. Chris spent a restless night after telling me I had to leave, but I left for work the following morning planning to leave soon. During that day at work, I received a phone call from Chris saying he had received a letter from our father suggesting that I could stay longer if I could find a place near them where they could keep in touch with me. I was given a reprieve from going home, but I still had to move out within a week. As I rode the bus from March Field to Riverside, I explored every possibility for another place to stay. Several sisters from Minnesota had an apartment and allowed me to move in by the end of the week, but for only one week. During this time I was able to find another place in the same complex, and I ended up sharing an apartment with two women who were a lot older than I was.

Family
Photographs

*The author's paternal grandparents Jens Andersen and Ane
Kirstine Laustdotter Andersen taken in the 1860s.*

The author's maternal grandparents, Johanne and Peder Christensen.

The author's mother's parents and six of her nine siblings. Standing in the back row from the left: sister Ane Kirstine and mother Johanne. Front row from left: sister Marie, brothers Jens, brother Herman, the author's mother, Mariane, brother John (aka Peter Johannes) and the author's father, Peder Christian Christensen.

The author's father Anders Christian (Chris) Andersen and mother, Mariane Olivia Christensen ca 1890.

The author's father Anders Christian (Chris) Andersen in the Danish Calvary (standing on the right) with unidentified fellow soldiers. Chris acquired swordsmanship skills while serving in the military. His skills impressed his sons who fashioned their own swords from tree branches and practiced swordplay so they could impress their father.

This photograph was take in Iowa in 1918. In the back from the left: the author's maternal uncle John (aka, Peder Johannes Christensen), uncle John's daughter, Alice, the author's maternal aunt, Marie Christensen, the author's mother, Mariane, holding her son Henry, the author's brother Harold (standing below Henry), the author's father, Chris, and the author's sister, Esther.

The author's parents with seven of their ten children. From left to right: Harvey, Esther, Chris (the author's father), Eva, Harold, Ragnhild, Mariane (the author's mother), Henry (on his mother's lap) and Holger in 1918.

The author's father riding a horse in front of the house that the author's parents lived in after their return to Denmark from America in 1908.

This pendant (about three quarters of an inch wide and one quarter inch thick) was carved by the author's maternal grandfather, Peder Christensen, from a piece of amber found on the west coast of Denmark, ca 1907, while he was walking along the shore with Eva, the author's oldest sister. He took the amber back to his workshop and stood three year old Eva on an Apple box crate so she could watch her grandfather create the beautiful heart-shaped pendant. Eva's daughter Mary Ann has the pendant and wears it to this day.

This photograph was taken in 1902 showing the author's mother (seated) and father standing on the right. The author's paternal aunt, Mettine Pouline is on the left with a friend at her side.

From the left, the author's paternal uncle Lars (Lars Nielsen Andersen), aunt Tina (aka, Attine Marie Andersen), paternal grandfather Jens Andersen, aunt Pauline (aka, Mettine Pouline Andersen) and the author's father Chris, in 1914.

The author's father on the left with three of his seven siblings: Anders Poulsen, Dorthea and Niels (Niels changed his last name to Agdahl after achieving business success in Denmark). The author's father and his siblings were born between 1870 and 1887.

This photograph of the author's parents and their first two children, Eva and Ragnhild, was taken in Denmark in 1907. Eva (right) and Ragnhild (left) were born in America during the author's parents' first immigration. Their third and fourth children, Holger and Harvey, were born in Denmark after returning to their homeland. In 1908, they immigrated to America for the second time.

The author's parents, Anders Christian (Chris) and Mariane Olivia Andersen ca 1949. In this photograph, Chris is 73 years old and Mariane is 63 years old.

*The author's siblings Ragnhild, Eva and Holger on their way
to Bennett School in Missouri Valley, Iowa in 1911.*

The author's sister Esther holding the author in 1927.

The author (center, with the serious expression) and her three sisters, Ragnhild, Esther, and Eva in 1929.

The author (on the left) at 14 years old with her third grade teacher, Miss Petersen (stepdaughter of the author's uncle Otto), Marilyn Christensen (daughter of the author's uncle John) and Irene Christensen (daughter of the author's uncle Elias). The photograph was taken in Loveland, Iowa in 1941.

The author's six brothers ca 1928 (from the left): Chris, Holger,
Harold (above), Ken (below), Harvey and Henry.

This Andersen family photograph was taken in Missouri Valley, Iowa shortly after my father died on February 15, 1951. Shown standing are my brothers (from the left) Ken, Henry, Harvey, Harold, Chris and Holger. Seated in the front is the author, my sister Eva, my mother Mariane, and sisters Ragnhild and Esther.

The author's first husband, Horace Bartlett (Bart) Lane and the author in 1944. Bart was 21 years old and I was 17 years old in this photograph.

The author's first husband Bart Lane (standing on the left) with the crew of the B-24 in 1944.

The author and her second husband, William (Bill) J.
Love, taken in Boulder, Colorado in 1948.

*Marian and Bill about to dance at their 50th wedding
anniversary celebration August 23, 1997.*

Marian and Bill dancing in their daughter Judy's home in Oregon.

Part Three

My First Marriage

Shortly after moving in with my new roommates, I met Bart Lane, who also used the officers' swimming pool. He concluded that I needed swimming lessons, and I accepted his offer to teach me. He later saw me in the officers' club with Donna and came over to talk to us. Our next meeting was in San Bernardino, where I was shopping with Esther, one of my housemates. Bart was with his friend Bob Bonner and another girl. He left and returned shortly without the girl, who he told me was with his friend Bob. He later confessed that she was in fact with him. The four of us went bowling, and I impressed him with a score of 140. It was the first time I had ever gone bowling. From then on, we saw each other daily. He took me to dinner at the officers' club each evening, and we enjoyed each other's company immensely. He told me that he was waiting to be matched with a B-24 crew; he then would be sent overseas following a brief training period. A couple of weeks later, he was matched with a group, and I was very sad to learn that this meant he would shortly be headed overseas.

I had great admiration for Bart. He was very responsible and dependable, and he refrained from consuming liquor out of respect for me. Instead, we always had soft drinks together. I enjoyed his devotion to me, and I had never experienced such love before. It was truly a life-changing time. We decided to get married before he had to leave. After our wedding, we spent four weeks together before he shipped out. The day he left, he and everyone else who was leaving marched to the train, which had backed into the base several days before. Those of us who were there to kiss our loved ones good-bye were on the platform waiting for them. Bart and I were together possibly twenty minutes, holding each other close until it was time for him to leave. Betty Smarinsky, the wife of the B-24 pilot, had told me earlier that a good wife wouldn't cry. As she and I walked away, she said that I was a good wife.

The train took them to Hamilton Field in San Francisco, where they awaited further orders for the trip overseas. I spent the night with Betty and left for Iowa the next day. I felt extremely alone, like half of me was gone. Bart and I had been together every possible moment, and now we were separated and alone. The train ride home was a two-day trip by train to return to my parents and my high school, where I had to make up the month I had missed. Bart wrote me almost every day and called me often, but my life was very lonely. I spent hours writing letters to Bart. I was afraid that I would say something that might hint at the possibility he might not come back. I had no interest in taking part in any social activities. All I could think about was his safe return. Each night, I carried his picture from our piano to my bedroom.

I made up my schoolwork without any problem, while I worked at a local drugstore. It was about this time that I heard Bob Birch was missing, but I was so concerned about Bart that it did not sink in. I also wrote Bart's parents on a regular basis. Bart's mother, Dorotha Lane, planned to go to Montana to help her sister after the birth of her child. Bart wrote me to say that Dorotha would like to visit with me at that time. She also wrote me, and we made plans for her to visit early in March. I think she arrived on March 1. I took a bus to Omaha and met her at the train station. Dorotha and I took the bus back to

Missouri Valley. Everyone in my family and I liked her very much. She was very genuine and sincere. My parents were wonderful and did everything to make her feel comfortable. She, in turn, liked them.

On March 3 while she was still at our house, Dorotha had a terrible dream that Bart was extremely stressed and that something was terribly wrong. She said that ultimately, everything was very peaceful. On that same night, a German Messerschmitt Me 262 fighter plane flew through the B-24 formation, attacking the plane above Bart's plane. That plane fell onto Bart's plane, cutting off the tail and causing Bart's plane to pitch up and then fall back, spinning out of control and falling from the sky. The Germans had sent up as many fighter planes as they could that day because they knew they were losing the war and decided to make a desperate attempt to fight back. The turret gunner on Bart's plane, who bailed out, said he heard Bart telling the first pilot, "Irving, go down!" to avoid colliding with the plane above that was hit by the fighter.

We weren't notified about the plane crash until March 21. We hadn't received any letters from him for at least a week, and I was terribly concerned that something had happened. On the evening of March 21, 1945, our doorbell rang. As I reached for the telegram, I knew what had happened. I saw the word *missing* and fell to my knees, praying and pleading with God that the worst had not happened. In my mind, it couldn't be true.

The school year was almost over when the war in Europe finally came to an end. Soon after my graduation, plans were made for me to move to Seattle in late May to be with Bart's family. Before I left on May 3, 1945, two of Bart's crew members were released from German prison camps. Both of them had been thrown from the plane as it went down and somehow had survived. The bombardier recalled that the violent movement of the plane threw him against the nosepiece and out of the plane. The turret gunner had little recollection of what had happened except that he felt himself floating in midair. It was an unbearable thought that it was so close to the end of the war and Bart might not be coming back. I lived with the hope that he too had somehow survived and would return.

In May, I arrived in Seattle to be with Bart's family. They were eager to have me there with them as, together, we waited with the hope that Bart might be alive and, like his companions, would be released from some German prison camp. The summer passed slowly while all of us tried to think positively. As long as the report said, "missing," we could believe there was still hope.

Fall finally came. I was somewhat reluctant to start college. If Bart did come back, I did not want to be tied up in school. Horace, Bart's dad (I called him Dad Lane), told me it was very important for me to think of my future and that I should start attending the University of Washington that fall. I followed his suggestion and made a trip home to see my parents before college started. Classes started, and I studied hard, even though I was sick a lot of the time during my first semester. By the time the second semester started, I changed my major from science to nursing. I felt very good about having done that. I was very uncertain when I signed up for chemistry class, having never taken chemistry in high school, but I wanted to prove to myself that I could do it. In fact, I did well and received an A in chemistry.

After Bart had been missing for a year, we were informed, as we feared we would be, that the missing status had been changed to deceased. I couldn't bring myself to fully realize that he wasn't coming back. I was heartbroken. I told Dad Lane that I still thought there was hope, to which he answered, "No, he will not be coming home." I did not attend classes that day, even though Dad Lane urged me to do so. The only thing I had to console myself was the thought that there had to be someone out there who would be there for me to take Bart's place. As I watched the celebration of VJ Day in Seattle, it all seemed hollow to me.

Shortly after I finished my first year living with the Lanes, I went home to Iowa with plans to return in time for Bart's sister Charis's marriage. I hated to leave early to return to Charis's wedding and stayed on. Just before I was to return to Seattle in the fall, my father suggested it would be better for me to change to a different college and get a new start. I called the University of Colorado, and with my high grade point average, I was assured of being accepted. Bart's parents were wonderful to me. They packed up my clothes and sent them to me in time for me to leave for the University of Colorado.

I was assigned to a large dorm that had originally been an armory. I was extremely lonely and kept telling myself things would get better. After a few days, I met two girls who became very good friends. Nita was a junior majoring in premed, and Doris was a junior and a nursing major. Nita became the closest friend I had ever had. We still keep in touch. The three of us enjoyed the weekly dances, and I was adjusting well to my new situation. I was not able to get into a chemistry class to continue the one I had taken at the University of Washington, so I was short one semester, which left a gap in my understanding of chemistry. Doris left for nursing school in Denver after the first semester, but I still enjoyed having Nita as well as other friends.

I felt sad not being able to attend Bart's memorial service at Jefferson Barracks, Missouri, on October 3, 1949. On May 11, 1948, Dad Lane and Dorotha were informed that Bart's remains had been recovered and interred in the US military cemetery in Margraten, Holland. An investigation was under way to see if Bart's body could be positively identified. On May 4, 1949, a letter to Bart's parents said that his remains had been found, but that they were unable to positively identify him because of the manner in which he had died— in a midair collision with another plane, followed by an explosion. The crash occurred approximately forty miles north of Magdeburg. Of the nineteen crew members in the two B-24 planes that crashed, only three survived. The remains of fifteen of the crew members were buried in a common grave in a civilian cemetery in Magdeburg. The remains of another crew member, who died in a hospital, were interred at Salzwedel in Germany and were later transferred to the cemetery at Neuville-en-Condroz, Belgium. The group burial in the American cemetery in Margraten, Holland, left Bart and the others unable to be identified. The Jefferson Barracks National Cemetery was chosen for their burial in the United States, since it was located closest to their loved ones. The last letter I received in 1949 informed me that the final burial would be at Jefferson Barracks in St. Louis, Section 79, grave number 299. My second husband, Bill Love, and our first two daughters visited Bart's grave in 1950. I visited his grave again in 1966 when I attended the wedding of my nephew Jerry Linder, in St. Louis, Missouri. I hope to see the grave again, although I realize not much of Bart is there.

Part Four

My Second Marriage

In October 1946, I met my future second husband, Bill Love, at a Halloween dance in my dorm at the University of Colorado. I very quickly noticed him because he was quite tall. Since it was a broom dance, I gave his partner the broom and got to dance with him and engage him in conversation. I was impressed that he was teaching half time while he worked on his master's degree in engineering. My hope was that he would call me later. He did call me within a week, and we began dating. He said I looked sad, and he probably called me for that reason. I made an effort to accept every date when he called. The college closed a month before Christmas because a coal strike meant no heat. I thought a lot about him during the vacation, and he likewise thought about me. When we returned after Christmas, Bill gave me a beaded sterling silver necklace and told me of the affection he felt for me. After that, I didn't hear from him again for a month.

I began dating Joe Connelly, who was introduced to me by a friend named Lynn Hart. Lynn was dating Joe's roommate. Joe was wonderfully sweet to me and obviously liked me a lot, but I kept thinking about Bill. Finally, after a month had passed, I called Bill and I said we needed to talk. He came over and confessed that he was afraid of a commitment, and therefore had not called me. We started dating again and continued through the semester until it was time for me to complete my nursing degree at the medical school in Denver. Bill helped me move and went back to Boulder. Both of us realized that we were serious about each other but we were not dealing with the long-term situation. As Bill made weekly trips and began missing me more than he expected, and I was finding that I did not like to be separated from him, the notion of getting married became more plausible.

We made plans to go back to my home in Iowa in the middle of the summer to have our wedding, but Bill's dad suffered a heart attack and he thought that he might have to go home to take care of his mother and sister. The plans for our wedding dissolved. During this time, a former housemate of Bill's asked me out for a date. I told Bill about the call, and at that point, Bill suggested another wedding date. We traveled back to Iowa on August 21, 1947, and were married at my parents' house on August 23, with only a few family members attending. Our Methodist minister, whom I knew well (I sang in the church choir through most of high school), performed the ceremony.

The evening after the wedding, Bill and I returned to Denver, where I took the tests necessary to finish my nursing probation period. Bill was headed to San Diego in a few days to serve two weeks on a submarine for his navy reserve duty. I was to meet him in San Diego two weeks after I finished my exams. While I waited in Denver, I went to Boulder to straighten out our belongings at the dorm for married couples. The apartment complex had just been finished, and our apartment consisted of one room with a kitchen, a foldout bed, and a bathroom. As I tried to make some order out of our belongings, I found a picture of Bill's sister, whom I had yet to meet. Things seemed a bit foreign to me and not as exciting as I had hoped.

A few days later, I flew to San Diego, and Bill had told me that I was to take a taxi to the commander's address on Coronado Island. When I arrived, I met the commander's wife, who was about six months pregnant and had a darling son about two and a half years old. She and I had time to talk before our husbands returned that evening. She told me her first husband had been killed on a submarine mission and that she had married Bud Watkins, a friend of her former husband. Her son was the child of her first husband. Bill and Bud came in from submarine duty that evening, and I was very impressed by how handsome Bill looked in his navy uniform. We enjoyed the Watkins a lot. We stayed several nights with them. One evening, another couple was invited for dinner. After dinner, we played the feather game—a feather was tossed into the circle in which we sat, and we tried to blow it away from ourselves over the shoulder of another player, who would then have to remove an article of clothing. The three men's objective was to blow the feather over the shoulder of the other two spouses. Bill in his loyalty to me removed his bridged tooth to save me from embarrassment (a husband could help his spouse). Bud's wife was down to her panties and bra. I was relieved when the game finally ended.

The next day, Bud fixed us a wonderful meal, which I appreciated, but I asked Bill if we could see the sights of San Diego. He feared hurting the Watkins' feelings, so we never saw San Diego. My other recollection was the evening when the Watkins and we visited the naval officers' club. Bill met someone he knew during the time he'd been stationed there. Bill's friend laughed as he recalled Bill's time there. Bill insisted that he did not want to discuss it. His friend never revealed anything substantial, but the conversation made me very inquisitive. We left San Diego on the third or fourth day after I arrived and headed for Portland, where I was going to meet Bill's parents for the first time. As we left San Diego, I began feeling as if I might be pregnant.

We drove to Portland in Bill's 1936 De Soto sedan. When we arrived at his parents' home, I made Bill drive around the block twice while I got up enough nerve to meet his parents and his sister, Shirley. His parents and sister were eagerly awaiting our arrival. They were all very pleasant, and obviously we were all trying to put our best foot forward. We spent a week there before we left for Boulder to register for the next semester. We tried to cover as many miles each day as possible.

By now I was feeling quite nauseated. Bill's mother, Helen, had advised Bill to wait to have children but Bill replied that he thought it might be too late. She looked unnerved but maintained her composure, saying we should still be cautious.

I was going through feelings of sadness because I had hoped to see Bart's parents in the fall to attend a memorial service for Bart. I was hoping this would give me a sense of closure, which I thought would help the Lanes and me, as well as honor Bart. I wanted to call them while we were in Portland, but I felt too awkward to do so. As Bill and I left Portland, Bill stopped for gas, and I spotted a telephone. I hurried to the phone and quickly dialed the Lanes. Dorotha answered, but the conversation had to be short. I felt badly that there wasn't more time to talk with all of them. She told me to be sure to send them my new address, which I did. When we returned to the campus in Boulder, Bill was very busy preparing both for teaching as well as for the courses he was taking. I changed my major to home economics, but my heart was not in it. I was taking a light schedule, with courses in American history, literature, sewing, and archery. I was not taking any courses in medical science, which was my first love.

Bill continued on with his heavy schedule and so was usually gone in the evenings working on his special project in thermodynamics, part of his master's degree program. During the first month of school, I was sure I was pregnant. I fell asleep early in the evening, and Bill thought I needed to discipline myself more, commenting on how he had stood watch on submarines and had to discipline himself to stay awake.

After finishing my first semester, I discontinued my course work because I did not want to attend classes while I looked pregnant as well as feeling concerned that the baby's arrival would probably cut short the semester. I started an extension class but quickly became bored with it. In the evenings, I occasionally walked over to the office where Bill was working. I tossed rocks at the window to alert him that it was time to come home. I still had my close friend Nita but seldom saw her. Dean and Phyllis McFeron were friends whom I had met through Bill. They lived in a Quonset hut down the hill about a mile from us. They had a small child, David. Phyllis was very friendly, and occasionally we visited them. Neither of us thought we could afford telephones.

Bill and I would often go on drives on Sundays. I did not yet know how to drive. Bill gave me a few lessons, but I didn't practice very much. While he was in the hospital having hernia surgery, I was about six and a half months pregnant but decided I would surprise him by getting my driver's license. A friend from the apartments drove me to take the driving test in our De Soto. The kind man who tested me thought that my erratic driving was caused by my being nervous, and so he decided to pass me. The truth was I should not have been on the road or anywhere else. I was totally unprepared. I drove over to the hospital to surprise Bill, since I now had my driver's license. After I left the hospital, he noticed that I was driving up a road leading to the mountains. A short time later, Nita called him at the hospital saying that I was supposed to meet her and hadn't shown up. Bill could only surmise that I was stranded somewhere in the mountains. He nearly became apoplectic. Still recovering from his hernia surgery, he limped over to a phone and called our next-door apartment friend who had a telephone. I was home and came to the phone. Bill was beside himself and asked what had happened. As things turned out, Nita got our time wrong and I surprisingly got home safely. I was given orders that I wasn't to drive that car again, and did I understand!

Bill was allowed to come home after a few days, and I was soon driving regularly out of necessity. I bumped a fender or two but considered myself fortunate that nothing worse happened.

Jean was not due until June, but she arrived early. We went on a rugged mountain ride the night before she was born, but whether that caused my early delivery, we never knew for sure. My water started leaking during the night, and we decided to go to the hospital. We were doubtful that I would give birth so soon, so Bill left the hospital to go back to his classes. When he returned at around noon, I was very close to delivery. I gave birth shortly after he arrived. Since I felt smothered by the gas mask, I delivered Jean naturally in May 1948. Bill had wanted a boy, but he was thrilled to see Jean. He seemed to walk a foot off the ground. Phyllis and Dean saw him with his cigars walking up to their house. Bill looked so excited, she thought I had given birth to twin boys. I was also thrilled, and I remember looking in the mirror and telling myself that from now on, I had to set an example for Jean. Bill and I walked back to the nursery each day to admire her.

I had so much milk that she was above her birth weight before I went home. However, that all changed when the reality set in that I was totally responsible for Jean. I had no idea what I was supposed to do to bring in the milk. Instead of nursing often, I thought I needed to conserve it. Bill's mother, who visited us shortly after Jean's birth, was not helpful. She had been unsuccessful at nursing, and when Jean cried, she said that babies had to cry to develop their lungs. I had a baby scale, and Jean's weight was static. My doctor told me that bottle-feeding was just as healthy for the baby as breastfeeding. In fact, bottle-feeding seemed to be his preference so I supplemented Jean's feeding with a bottle. I was very nervous and fearful about my responsibilities, and Bill became very unstrung. He ended up dropping a class in which he was receiving straight As.

Because our apartment was for couples only, we had to move when Jean was a month old. We moved into former army barracks and stayed there until Bill finished his master's degree in the fall. We then moved to Temple City, California, where Bill started his PhD program at the California Institute of Technology. As a result of the polio scare, I flew to Portland with Jean, who was now four months old. I stayed there for a couple of weeks while Bill went on another submarine cruise. Once again, we had to stay in military housing. This time it was a two-story army barracks.

Jean and I spent a lot of time together. We would go on a couple of walks each day. Bill was once again teaching part-time. Being unaware of how difficult courses were at Caltech, he took a much too heavy course load. He spent all of his time studying when he wasn't in classes. We were very fortunate to have Bill's aunt Emily and uncle Charlie there. Aunt Emily had two nephews and two married children who lived near them. They formed what she called, "the gang." Every holiday, we got together. I think my life would have been very dismal if it hadn't been for Aunt Emily.

When Jean was eight months old, I became pregnant with Judy. As the year progressed, Bill became more and more discouraged and realized he would have to leave Caltech. Dean McFeron went to the University of Illinois when he left school at Boulder and was helpful in arranging a contact at that university, where Bill was able to transfer.

Bill became sick just before we were scheduled to leave Temple City, in June 1949, so it was touch-and-go getting our trailer packed and leaving. Dear Aunt Emily invited us to stay the last night at her house, where she prepared a delicious dinner. We left the next morning, pulling a heavy trailer. The backseat of our Ford, which we had bought in Boulder, was packed in such a way that Jean could sleep in the back while we traveled. The engine overheated on the El Cajon Pass, so we had to do our driving at night.

When we arrived in Portland, Bill's parents greeted us with open arms. They were a little embarrassed that we had all of our possessions in a trailer. She believed that was a negative indication of our social status. Bill's mother was also worried because Jean wanted to stay close to me, so she decided that Jean had to go outside and stay in a playpen. I was not able to stand my ground, and Jean was left in the playpen to cry frantically. In desperation, Jean climbed out and crawled across the lawn to try to find me. Her grandmother was dismayed and wondered how I would ever manage to raise both Jean and another baby.

Our plan was for me to stay in Portland after Bill left to go to Illinois. I would give birth in Portland and then move to Illinois when our second daughter, Judy, was a month old. However, Grandma and I did not do well together. She wanted to tell me how I was supposed to plan and do everything, and she complained about me to Bill. I wrote my mother to see if I could go to Iowa to have Judy instead of staying in Portland. She agreed, and we decided I would fly to Iowa with Jean, and Bill would drive to Illinois pulling the trailer.

After I arrived in Iowa, it became apparent that my mother was not up to the task of having me stay with her. My father had developed Alzheimer's, and things were very difficult for her. Bill drove to Illinois as soon as the situation became obvious to him. He was desperate to find housing, since I was due to give birth in six weeks. Judy was born a month after Jean and I arrived in Illinois. A friend of Bill's from Caltech had a grandmother who lived in Urbana, and Bill had stopped by to see her. She told him there might be a place for us to live across the street with a seventy-eight-year-old gentleman named Mr. Ray, who recently had a couple staying with him. He agreed that we could stay with him. It felt like a miracle that we found the place. After moving in, I assumed the responsibility for keeping house and cooking for Mr. Ray, who was still working. After I heard from Bill that he had found housing, Jean and I left the following morning on a train from Missouri Valley; the train arrived in Chicago that evening. I needed to transfer to another station. Jean was unbelievably good throughout the trip. She jumped out of her seat to play with me as we boarded the train that left from Missouri Valley. I firmly told her that she had to stay in her seat and I asked her emphatically, "Do you understand?" She never again left her seat.

After I made the transfer in Chicago, Jean was asleep, and I carried her and my suitcase to board the next train. I was amazed that no one offered to help me. I arrived in Champaign Urbana at three in the morning, and Bill was there to meet me and take us to our new home. We were now both very relieved. It was an old house built around the turn of the century, but it was in a pleasant neighborhood of older people and large trees. It reminded me of Iowa, which made the adjustment easier. The house had no facilities for washing clothes. We bought a washing machine, which we rolled from the pantry to the small kitchen sink, where we could pump out the wash water. In order to rinse the clothes, we had to fill the washer a second time and add back the clothes. We used a clothesline outside, but there was no place to hang the clothes if the weather was rainy or freezing. A kind lady next door offered us the use of her basement to dry our clothes during bad weather. We had one bathroom upstairs and a potty chair downstairs for Jean. There were three bedrooms upstairs, one for Mr. Ray, one for Jean, and one for Bill and me.

I was due to deliver in six weeks, but Judy was born only a month after I arrived in Illinois. We found a physician through Phyllis McFeron, but there was no one to watch Jean. Somehow, we located a very dear woman, Maggie Richman, who was able to stay at our place while I was hospitalized. She stayed on for a couple of weeks after Judy was born. She was like a mother to me and took good care of Jean, the house, and the cooking. I felt sad when she had to leave. Bill and I did the wash three days a week, early in the morning before he had to leave for school. I had a diaper service for the extras that we couldn't get washed.

Judy was a darling baby and very good. I remember how she smiled at my expressions early on. She suffered from colic in the early evening for the first couple of months but otherwise was wonderful. I used the very large padded dining table for a bed so she could see the room and us as well as be near me. This worked well until I had surgery after Christmas, when she was three months old. College was in recess, and Bill was taking care of both Jean and Judy while he studied. Judy had been crying for some time, but Bill was engrossed in his schoolwork and never checked to see why she was crying. She scooted on her heels backward, and when he finally looked up, it was too late to catch her as she hung over the end of the table and fell to the floor. He didn't dare tell me what had happened until I got home from the hospital.

Jean was very affectionate with Judy and enjoyed any contact she could have with her. In the evening, she would squeeze in beside Mr. Ray while he listened to *The Lone Ranger* on the radio. Mr. Ray was a very kind and pleasant man. The meals I made were rather simple, but he never complained.

As spring approached, I was not healing well from my surgery and we realized I needed easier conditions in which to live. We were eventually able to move into army barracks that the university offered to veterans' families. We hated to leave Mr. Ray. He had been very kind, but we broke the news to him before Bill left for a two-week submarine cruise assignment. While Bill was gone, Mr. Ray learned that he had colon cancer and left to live with his son in Indiana. He never returned and died shortly thereafter. We moved to the barracks about one block from our friends the McFerons. There were many children for Jean and Judy to play with. We bought an automatic washing machine and hung our clothes on a collapsible dryer during bad weather. Jean and Judy were sick quite a lot after our move, perhaps in part because they had not previously been exposed to more children.

When the Korean War started, one of the men on Bill's recent cruise was called back into service. Bill and I both feared that he would be called back as well, and since we had also talked about having three children close together, we decided now was the time to have our third child. Nancy was born in April 1952, one day before Bill's birthday.

Bill was now frantically studying to complete his PhD by the end of summer. He would call to tell me when he was coming home for dinner so I would have it ready for him. Bill sometimes used the expression "Knock it off" when he wanted things to settle down. Hearing this, Judy told Nancy to "knock it down" during one of the meals when Nan was crying. By the middle of the summer, I was told that I needed another gastrointestinal surgery. The prior surgery had not healed well. Once again, our dear friend Maggie came to take care of the three girls while I was hospitalized.

By the end of the summer, Bill completed his PhD, so we packed up and left to go to Richland, Washington, where Bill was going to work for General Electric on plutonium-producing reactors. After we left Illinois, we stopped at my mother's house on our way west. We then continued our drive across the country. The girls and I stayed at Bill's parents' house until he was able to find a three-bedroom home in Richland. We left Portland in time to celebrate Thanksgiving in Richland with Bill. Our three daughters and I had stayed in Portland for nearly three months.

We lived in Richland for three years, then moved to Los Gatos, California in the fall of 1955, where Bill began his next job at the new power division for Commonwealth Edison's nuclear reactor. A year later, we moved again, to Denver, Colorado, where Bill became an associate professor at the University of Denver and a senior research engineer for the Denver Research Institute. He eventually divided his time between working at the Denver Research Institute and Sundstrand Turbo and Hydraulics Machinery, also in Denver.

When our first son, Billy, was born in 1959, we were ecstatic. Bill's father, Grandpa Love, actually popped a button on his suit jacket as he literally swelled with pride after hearing about Billy's birth. A year later, we moved back to Richland, and not finding the home we wanted, we decided to build. We acted as our own contractor and landscaped our yard. Richland was very hot during the summer but we enjoyed swimming in the city pool and entertaining on our large patio. We were able to enjoy skiing during most winters. In April 1962, our fifth child, Steve, was born. He was a delight to all of us and soon established a close relationship with his father. Because Steve had significant health issues as a baby, I was very concerned about his well-being, devoting considerable time trying to restore his health. It was only after we moved to Schenectady that a doctor there was able to manage his digestive problems. Steve offered all of us great fun, was compliant and loved taking walks with me. We often brought a carrot to a horse named Tex which was owned by a high school friend of Judy.

Jean and Judy went to college and were married while our family lived in New York. Nancy started college and Billy and Steve relocated with us one more time, to Seattle, Washington, in 1970, where Bill became a full professor of mechanical engineering at the University of Washington. Happily, our three daughters later moved to the Northwest as well. The move to Seattle was difficult, particularly for our son Billy, who was entering the seventh grade. In addition, Bill and I were growing older as we faced new challenges in the tumultuous decade of the 1970s.

Christmas was one time of year when most of our family reunited in Seattle. As more grandchildren arrived, our youngest daughter, Nancy, treated us to wonderful gourmet Christmas Day dinners.

Bill eventually retired from the navy as a lieutenant commander after twenty-six years of service. In 1983, he also retired as a professor from the University of Washington. In January 2007, Bill died shortly after he was diagnosed with lymphoma. Once again, I had lost the love of my life and knew things would be forever changed. I continue to miss him each day. We fell in love all over again after his retirement. We were married for almost sixty years. I stayed in Seattle for four years and in 2010, moved to Portland near my daughter Jean and her family and three of Judy's sons and their families.

Appendix A

Author's Parents, Grandparents, Aunts & Uncles	Born	Died
Father Anders Christian Andersen	Jan 6, 1876 (Skøttrup Børglum, DK)	Feb 15, 1951 (Missouri Valley, Iowa)
Father's grandfather Anders Poulsen	1805 (Denmark, farmer)	May 7, 1867 (Denmark)
Father's grandmother Mette Christinedotter	1807 (Denmark)	?
Father's father Jens Andersen	Apr 29, 1847 (Denmark)	Aug 29, 1921 (Mo Valley, IA)
Father's mother Ane Kirstine Laustdotter	Oct 12, 1843 (Denmark)	Jan 28, 1897 (Denmark)
Father's brother Anders Poulsen Andersen	Oct 31, 1870 (Denmark)	?
Father's sister Dorthea Andersen	Jan 13, 1874 (Skøttrup Børglum, DK)	?
Father's brother Lars Nielsen Andersen	Feb 15,1872 (Skøttrup Børglum, DK)	Sept 6, 1940 (Clarinda, IA)
Father's brother Martin Christensen Andersen	Sept 12, 1878 (Hundelev, Jelstrup, DK)	Ca 1892 (US)
Father's brother Niels Agdahl (né Andersen)	Dec 21, 1880 (Hundelev, Jelstrup, DK)	Dec 6, 1942 (Hundelev, Jelstrup, DK)
Father's sister Mettine Pouline Andersen	Jun 3, 1884 (Denmark)	1961 (Denmark)
Father's sister Attine Marie Andersen	Jun 28, 1887 (Hundelev, Jelstrup, DK)	?
Mother Mariane Olivia Christensen	Jun 11, 1885 (Denmark)	May 13, 1974 (Strawberry Point, IA)

Mother's father Peder Christian Christensen	Jun 12, 1857 (Denmark)	Oct 13, 1937 (Denmark)
Mother's mother Johanne Christensen	Nov 16, 1858 (Denmark)	Mar 22, 1931 (Denmark)
Mother's sister Ane Kirstine (Stine) Christensen	Jun 4, 1879 (Denmark)	1961 (Denmark)
Mother's sister Marie Christensen	Oct 25, 1883 (Denmark)	?
Mother's sister Eva Christensen	1904 (Denmark)	?
Mother's brother Jens Christian (Chris) Christensen	Oct 11, 1881 (Denmark)	1954 (Denmark)
Mother's brother Herman Axel Frederik Christensen	Apr 24, 1888 (Denmark)	1952 (Denmark)
Mother's brother Gudmund Christensen	1898 (Denmark)	?
Mother's brother Elias Emanuel Christensen	Mar 25, 1893 (Denmark)	Jul 1975 (Bellingham, Washington)
Mother's brother Peder J. (John) Christensen	Jun 1, 1890 (Denmark)	? (Lummi Island, WA)
Mother's brother Otto Aniamus Christensen	Nov 19, 1895 (Denmark)	? (Missouri Valley, IA)

Appendix B

Author's Siblings	Born	Died
Eva Kirstine	Sep 22, 1904 (Mo. Valley, IA)	Jan 8, 1994 (Omaha, NE)
Ragnhild Alma	Apr 1, 1907 (Mo. Valley, IA)	Dec 11, 1993 (Omaha, NE)
Holger Martin	May 19, 1909 (Denmark)	Dec 16, 1988 (Naples, FL)
Harvey Arthur	Jun 22, 2011 (Denmark)	May 9, 1983 (Santa Cruz, CA)
Harold Kermit	Sep 12, 1913 (farm near Mo. Valley, IA)	Dec 26, 1998
Esther Marie	Nov 15, 1915 (farm near Mo. Valley, IA)	Jul 24, 1992 (Council Bluffs, IA)
Henry Ellis	Nov 25, 1917 (farm near Mo. Valley, IA)	Aug 2, 1987
Chris Jr. Elmer	Jan 26, 1920 (farm near Mo. Valley, IA)	Feb 4, 1980 (Center Point, IA)
Kenneth Niels	1924 (farm near Mo Valley, IA)	—

Index

A

Agdahl 16, 95, 127
Allen, Howard 35
Anders 3, 16, 87, 95, 97, 127
Andersen 3, 5, 16, 26, 31, 33, 60,
  76, 87-8, 94, 97, 103, 127
Andrew 23
Ane 5, 7, 17, 86, 127
Anna 19
Ardelle 35, 56-7, 67
Attine 11, 94, 127

B

B-24 69, 81, 105, 109-11, 113
Barbara 35, 48-9
barracks 70, 113, 120, 123
Bart 10, 69, 104-5, 109-14, 118
Belgium 113
Betty 110
Bill 12, 16, 45, 49, 70, 106-8,
  114-25
Billy 125
Birch 80, 110
Børglum 3, 127
Boulder 106, 116-18, 121
Buer 71

C

Caltech 120-2
Carey 23, 34, 80

Cedar Rapids 76
Chicago 48, 59, 122
Chisman 81
Chris 3, 9, 15, 18, 28, 47, 61-2, 65-
  72, 75, 80-2, 87-90, 94, 97,
  102-3, 128-9
Christian 3-4, 8, 11, 17, 86-7, 97,
  127-8
Christinedotter 127
Colorado 106, 112-13, 115, 124
Coronado Island 116
Council Bluffs 28, 57-8, 81, 129
Crowder 44, 76

D

Denver 113, 116, 124-5
Denver Research Institute 124-5
Donna 68-71, 81-2, 109
Dorthea 95, 127

E

Edmundson 28
Elias 4, 17, 19, 101
Emily 120-1
Epworth Hospital 43
Eric 59
Esther 27-8, 33, 39, 43, 48, 56-60, 65,
  89-90, 99-100, 103, 109, 129
Eva 4, 10-14, 16-17, 20-4, 26-9, 33-
  7, 39, 47, 50, 56-7, 63, 67, 72,
  92, 96

F

Fredricks 68
Frode 18
Fuhrs 49

G

General Electric 124
Germany 44, 113
Gertler 18
Gillette's Dairy 46-8, 63
Grant 63-4
Great Depression 31, 42, 47, 50, 52, 54, 61-2, 72
Greta 18
Gudmund 4, 17

H

Hamilton Field 110
Harold 25-9, 34, 37, 46, 50-5, 57, 60-1, 63, 65-6, 73, 79, 89-90, 102-3, 129
Haroldine 34
Harvey 16, 19-21, 23, 28, 46-51, 61, 63, 67, 71, 90, 96, 102-3, 129
Hedevig 16
Henry 6, 28, 39, 47-8, 52-3, 60-8, 72, 74, 89-90, 102-3, 129
Herman 4, 17, 86
Holger 14-16, 20-8, 33, 36, 38-9, 41-5, 51, 57-8, 62, 68, 73-6, 90, 96, 98, 102-3
Holland 113
Hopkins, Johns 76

I

Illinois 70, 121-4
Indiana 43, 123
Iowa 1, 10, 12-13, 21, 33-4, 39, 42-3, 46, 57-8, 62-3, 68, 70-1, 75-6, 116, 121-2
Irving 111
Isenberger 62

J

Jean 70, 119-26
Jefferson 113
Jenny 28
Jensen 16, 19, 28-9, 37
Joan 58-9
Job's Daughters 80-1
Johanne 17, 85-6, 128
John 4, 17, 43, 46, 51, 58-9, 86, 89, 101, 128
Joplin 44
Judy 108, 121-6
Julia 9-12, 21, 23
Jutland 3-4

K

Karen 7, 62-3
Ken 10, 27-9, 34, 36, 38, 45, 47, 53, 56-8, 61-7, 70-80, 102-3
Kenneth 17, 63, 72, 76, 129
Kirklands 24
Kirstine 5, 7, 16-17, 33, 86, 127, 129

L

lane 28, 52, 69, 104-5, 109-10, 112-13
Lars 9-13, 21, 23-4, 94, 127

Laustdotter 5, 127
LaVonne 35, 56-7
Linder 58, 114
Logan 39, 63-4
Lønstrup 3, 18
Los Gatos 124
Love 4, 6, 8, 13, 48, 51-2, 57-8, 62, 64-6, 70-1, 80-2, 110, 114-16, 118, 124-6
Loveland 12, 52, 74, 101
Lynn 63, 115

M

Magdeburg 113
Maggie 17, 123-4
March Field 68, 81-2
Margraten 113
Marian 4, 6, 34, 36, 38, 40, 42, 44, 48, 52, 54, 58, 62, 78, 107-8
Mariane 3, 7, 86, 89-90, 97, 103, 127
Marie 4, 7, 11, 17-18, 46, 56, 86, 89, 94, 127, 129
Marilyn 17, 76-7, 101
Martin 8, 41, 80, 127, 129
Mary Ann 14, 35, 39, 47, 92
McFeron 118, 121, 123
meat hooks 70
Mette 127
Mettine 11, 93-4, 127
Minnie 7
Missouri Valley 10, 21, 23, 28, 33-4, 39, 46, 48, 51, 58, 63, 74-5, 98, 122, 127-8
Moorhead 29, 33-4, 37
Morningside 42, 48, 62, 68

N

Nancy 49, 54, 124-5
Nebraska 69
Nelson 35, 63, 75, 79
Neuville-en-Condroz 113
Niels 16, 72, 95, 127, 129
Nita 113, 118-19
Norma 54, 70-1
Nuclear 124

O

Omaha 25, 28, 35, 42, 47-8, 54, 61, 63, 67, 110, 129

P

Portland 117-18, 120-1, 124, 126
Pouline 11, 93-4, 127
Poulsen 16, 95, 127

R

Ragnhild 12, 14, 19-24, 26-9, 33-4, 37-40, 43, 57, 90, 96, 98, 100, 103, 129
Ray 55, 122-3
Richard 38-9
Richland 124-5
Robert's Dairy 47-8, 63

S

Salzwedel 113
San Diego 116-17
Santa Cruz 46, 49, 129
Schenectady 125
Scøttrup 3
Seattle 49, 71, 111-12, 125-6
Shirley 117

Sioux City   42, 62, 68
Skeesix   52
Smarinsky   110
Sorenson   18
South Bend   43
St. Louis   59, 113-14
St. Luke's   76
Stan   48
Stella   28, 39, 48, 62-4, 74
Steve   49, 125
Strawberry Point   36, 39, 43-5, 127

T

Tage   16-17
Ted   29, 34, 37, 39, 70
Temple City   120-1
Tina   8, 11, 94

U

University of Colorado   112-13, 115
University of Iowa   42, 46, 68, 71, 75-6
University of Pennsylvania   76
University of Washington   69, 112-13, 125

V

Viola   36, 43-5, 58, 68, 75

W

Washington   39, 69, 112-13, 124-5, 128
Watkins   117
Watts   43
Wilma   28, 46-9, 61, 67
World War II   4, 10, 16, 18, 31, 68